Learn and Play
the Recycle Way:
Homemade Toys
that Teach

Rhoda Redleaf • Audrey Robertson

Redleaf Press

Published by: Redleaf Press
                   a division of Resources for Child Caring, Inc.
                   450 North Syndicate, Suite 5
                   St. Paul, MN 55104

Distribubted by: Gryphon House
                   Mailing address:
                   PO Box 207
                   Beltsville, MD 20704-0207

Library of Congress Cataloging-in-Publication Data

Redleaf, Rhoda.
    Learn and play the recycle way : homemade toys that teach / Rhoda
Redleaf and Audrey Robertson.
        p.   cm.
    ISBN 1-884834-40-X
    1. Toy making. 2. Educational toys. 3. Recycling (Waste, etc.)
    I. Robertson, Audrey S. II. Title.
    TT174.R42 1999
    793—dc21   99-29587
                                                         CIP

Acknowledgments

The wealth of homemade ideas in this book and its predecessors, *Teachables from Trashables* and *Teachables from Trashables II*, is a tribute to the creativity and energy of the wonderful child care teachers, family child care providers, trainers, and others who make up the Minnesota child care community. Many of these ideas have been developed and shared over the years in classes, workshops, and conferences at Resources for Child Caring and elsewhere, and we wish to acknowledge and thank the many past and present staff members, trainers, and caregivers who have indirectly contributed to this book. Some of the ideas may have "morphed" somewhat as we have adapted them to take advantage of present day technology, but a little of the original "classic" ideas will always remain.

We also wish to thank those who have been directly involved in the production of this book. Paul Woods did a remarkable job of solving the huge layout and design problems. He fit over 100 ideas into an attractive and accessible book. Editor Rosemary Wallner did a beautiful job of making sure all our ideas, instructions, and inventions would be understandable to all. It was a pleasure working with Fredrik Hausmann, copy editor, who kept an eye on the endless details. Perhaps the most formidable task of all confronted Maria Young, who indexed all of the ideas in this book. Eileen Nelson, director of Redleaf Press, is always a joy to work with, and she calmly and efficiently solved every little or big issue that came along. Thank you one and all for your outstanding work.

Finally, thank you to our husbands for their support, encouragement, and good humor during the disruptions our work sometimes created—and to our grandchildren for inspiring and testing many of these ideas.

Contents

Introduction

A Look at Learning

Much has been written in recent years about the importance of learning in early childhood. Unfortunately, a trend to push for earlier and earlier *academic* learning has been the result. In reaction to this, the National Association for the Education of Young Children (NAEYC) has adopted a strong position statement for developmentally appropriate practice in working with young children. This position emphasizes the importance of play in fostering learning.

Young children learn through direct hands-on manipulation of their environment and a great deal of repetition. They learn best if they are at play and the learning emerges as a byproduct of that play. You can enhance the learning environment by asking questions, making associations between known and unknown, and stimulating interest and curiosity through toy selection and activities offered. You don't, however, need a constant flow of new toys. Often, reorganizing or adding to familiar toys and activities reawakens a child's interest.

The items described in this book are intended to be used in play—and in that sense they are toys. But these items also provide stimulation for major developmental and learning processes. The many skills that are involved in this growth and development process are often grouped into the following five broad areas:

1. *Physical development skills* are learned through the body and include large (gross) and small (fine) muscle movement.

2. *Sensory perception development skills* use the five senses, alone or in combination, and are crucial in learning to recognize and distinguish everything around us.

3. *Social and emotional development skills* deal with feelings, getting along with other people, understanding oneself and one's community, and being able to help oneself.

4. *Cognitive development skills* are those learned through the mind and include all the "thinking" skills, such as language (speaking, reading, writing), reasoning, problem solving, understanding basic concepts, organizing processes, math, and science.

5. *Creative development skills* add the dimension of some intangible elements of "spirit" or aesthetics to the cognitive and sensory processes that are involved in imagination, artistic or dramatic appreciation, and dramatic expression.

All of these skills are referred to frequently throughout *Learn and Play the Recycle Way* in the "What It Does" section of each activity.

Most toys included in this book serve multiple purposes, and you can use them in many different ways. This book suggests a few ways, and you and the children will discover many more. Feel free to exchange or substitute activities among toys of similar types.

A few general suggestions may help you in maximizing some of the learning potential:

- Understand that repetition is a necessary part of learning. Activities that quickly may bore adults often continue to be of interest to children. Many of the toys and games may strike you as versions of "the same old thing." To children, however, each one is a new experience—and it is the children's enjoyment that is the most important consideration.

- Vary the difficulty of matching games by making the discrimination tasks more complex or very simple to match the ability levels of the children involved in the activity.

- Capitalize on the interests of the children. For example, a child who has no interest in matching games but who loves dinosaurs will often participate willingly if the "matches" are of different types of dinosaurs. A child's attention span grows directly in relation to his or her interest in the activity.

- Present one skill or task at a time. Many matching games in this book include multiple matching criteria. This is to make the game more versatile in the long run, but initially, emphasize one criteria (for example, color). Generally, older children will show interest in the more complicated multiple criteria tasks.

- Recognize the "literacy" value of cue cards. These cards not only serve as "clues" to playing a game, but they also introduce the concept of symbols representing meaning, a pre-reading skill.

- Children's learning about games with rules is a slowly

evolving process. Young children frequently agree to rules but have no idea how to follow them and are not at all interested in the process. Avoid too many rules or "real games" that feature winners and losers.

- For young children, language helps to organize and interpret thought, action, and information. The say-along verses accompanying each toy introduce and explain some of the learning possibilities in that activity.

- The toys in this book can be adapted to incorporate elements of various cultures. For example, words from other languages can be included in some of the board games and counting or matching activities. In addition, you may find this book useful for working with and including parents in your curriculum, training new child care providers, training students or staff, and creating or augmenting your toy supply.

This book was written to help people who care for children understand and enjoy the learning potential inherent in play. Cherish the creativity and imaginative playfulness of childhood and appreciate its value for adults as well.

How to Use This Book

The different toys and activities included in this book are grouped into six age-related sections that range from infants to schoolagers. Sections one through five follow an age-related continuum from infants through schoolagers and allow for considerable overlapping. In general, the more versatile and flexible the item is the broader its age-related appeal. Section four is the only section to target a single age group, the preschoolers (children roughly three to five years old). The activities in this section focus on specific cognitive skills that are developing during the preschool years. The last section includes items that can be used with all ages. Our age-related suggestions should not be taken as absolutes, however. As you work with each child on a daily basis, you will best be able to ascertain each child's developmental readiness, interests, and experiences, all of which will greatly influence how and when an activity will be useful for that child.

Each toy or activity includes a say-along verse, which is a poem or fingerplay that can be used to introduce the item. The say-along verse helps to describe the item and its use and offers an ideal way to incorporate a language learning experience. You may want to copy the say-along verse onto a card for handy reference.

The "What You Need" section offers a list of materials needed, and "How to Make It" gives you step-by-step directions for making the toy. In some cases we have included alternative materials, variation games, or related activities.

Also included with each activity are two descriptive sections. The "What It Does" section describes the developmental skills each activity enhances. The "How to Use It" section describes activities and ways children of different ages might use the toy. Our suggested uses are just the beginning. We hope you will use your own creativity and encourage the children to use theirs to expand on the many possible uses of these items.

Helpful Hints for Making Your Own Toys

Once you have chosen a toy to make, carefully read through the "What You Need" and "How to Make It" instructions. Note any safety considerations, particularly if infants or toddlers will be using the finished product (use safe substitute materials if you prefer). Generally, you'll find that the suggested tools and materials are readily available to everyone.

Following are suggestions about selecting and using materials for toy making.

Glue. All-purpose white glues are usually marked "nontoxic" and, if so, are good for toy making. Many other glues contain substances that could be harmful if swallowed or inhaled, so be sure to check labels. Choose a brand that is marked "nontoxic." Glue sticks are generally nontoxic and are handy to use for many projects.

Felt-Tip Markers. Markers add color and are easy to use, but they do have limitations. Permanent markers are usually toxic and should be avoided. Water-based markers are usually safe, but toys made with them should be covered with clear contact paper to avoid bleeding should they become wet. When making infant or toddler toys, use contact paper cut in shapes instead of markers.

Contact Paper. Using contact paper in toy construction allows for easy cleaning and may increase the life of the toy. Brightly colored contact paper also helps attract a child's attention to the toy. Usually found in a variety of hardware or general retail stores, contact paper is a good investment for any serious toy maker. Pattern contact papers can be used in the same way as wrapping paper (see below). If the object or toy is flat, lamination is an alternative way to protect and preserve. Here is how to use contact paper:

1. Measure and cut the amount needed. Lay the piece flat on a table with covering side up.

2. Twist edges to loosen the covering.

3. Carefully peel away the covering and leave the contact paper on the table with the sticky-side up.

4. Lay items to be covered facedown on the contact paper. If needed, place a second piece of contact paper on top of the game pieces, sticky-side down.

5. Smooth by rubbing it with your fingers, then cut out the pieces. For single-side coverage, fold edges over the sides of the game piece or artwork.

Coding Dots. Coding dots come in all sizes and colors and are generally available in office supply stores. They usually come in boxes of 1,000 dots per color, so find other people who would like to share materials. Some craft shops and teacher supply stores have mixed colors of dots or labels, and some office supply stores sell individual sheets or smaller packages.

Wrapping Paper. Wrapping paper is useful for making puzzles and many kinds of matching games. Use new or used wrapping paper and look for attractive papers with six to eight or more repeated picture items. Use paper with an overall scene (such as a playground or a forest) or papers designed with all different kinds of items (such as trucks, rocket ships, animals, or flowers) repeated many times.

Plastic Containers and Lids. You can use all sizes and shapes of containers and lids for making and storing games. For ease in cutting plastic, heat the scissors or knife over a flame. The heat melts the plastic and makes it easier to cut. Cutting this way also produces a smooth edge on the plastic that is safe and looks good. Only adults should cut plastic in this way, and they should only do so in a well-ventilated area. Flames and sharp knives are not safe for children to use.

Juice Can Lids. Juice can lids work especially well in many toddler toys or matching games. Use only the smooth edge lids that come from pull-tab containers (popular on frozen juice cans). Glue pictures to the lids or use them in play as anything from play, money to "pancakes." Let the children invent uses.

Empty Tape Rolls. Use plastic or paper tape rolls as wheels, in a ring toss game, or in other imaginative ways.

Stickers and Seals. Children love stickers and will be happy just to stick them in books. You can convert stickers into matching or board games by using assorted stickers, such as ones with a holiday or animal theme. Look for at least six different versions of the same category (for example, six pumpkins or six butterflies). Look for books of stickers in teacher supply stores, instrument and sheet music stores, party shops, and drugstores. (Stickers found in party shops or drugstores usually cost more, so make sure the packages contain more than one sheet of each sticker.)

Magnetic Tape. Magnetic tape is a helpful product to use when making toys. One side of magnetic tape is adhesive, like regular tape, and the other side is magnetic. This tape is generally available in hobby shops, craft shops, and hardware stores. Remember that magnetic products of any kind must be kept far away from computers to avoid damage.

Velcro. Velcro is a self-gripping material that is a marvelous addition to toy making. Small pieces of Velcro added to matching games allow the parts to be matched without slipping and sliding out of place. Children can then carry the completed game around to show an adult. They can remove the Velcroed game pieces when they stop working or no longer want to play. Just remember that in using Velcro, the "smooth" or "loop" part must be on one side of the toy and the "teeth" or "hook" part must be on the other for the gripping to work.

Tagboard. Tagboard can be found in many office, art, or teacher supply stores. Recyclable alternatives that work equally well are used file folders, backs of tablets or coloring books, shirt or stocking inserts, cereal boxes, or any other type of lightweight cardboard.

Finding Materials for Toy Making

Discount stores, craft stores, outlet shops, hardware stores, and fabric and home decorating stores are all good sources for materials to use in toy making. Ask the managers of these stores to save usable surplus or unsold items for you. Parents are another good source for securing large amounts of common household items or recyclable materials.

Surplus stores are a good source for some items, but browsing and sorting through their supplies requires careful looking and time. A valuable resource for educators is Creative Educational Surplus, based in Eagan, Minnesota. This company has developed its business from doing that judicious searching out of the surplus items caregivers find so useful (such as Velcro, magnetic tape, Mylar papers, and many items used to make the toys in this book). Call 1-800-886-6428 for a catalog.

Safety Considerations in Making and Using Toys

Always consider the safety needs of children when you make toys. Safe toys for children meet the following tests:

- *They are clean.* Thoroughly wash and rinse all materials and containers before using.

- *They have no sharp parts.* Tape or round off corners. Take special care in removing lids from metal cans to be sure they are smooth along the rim. (You can often accomplish this by running the can opener around the can several times.) Sand and oil all material that might splinter.

- *They are too big to swallow.* For infants, toddlers, or any children who put non-food items in their mouths, the general rule is that an object be—at the very least—1 x 1½ inches in size. If you must use small objects, tie a few of them together to make them bigger. When using sponges or sponge-type materials in infant and toddler projects, cover items with sheer panty hose to prevent children from biting off pieces and choking on them. Do not use staples in toys you are making for infants and toddlers. If toddlers will be handling the toys you create, sewing or taping is much safer.

- *They are made of nontoxic materials.* Do not use any material that could be harmful if touched, eaten, chewed, or smelled. Read package instructions to make sure that markers, paints, and glue or other adhesives are nontoxic and safe for children (and adults) to use. Do not use Styrofoam pellets or packing materials in toys that toddlers will use. When toddlers are using blocks of Styrofoam, cover the blocks with contact paper to avoid small pieces from breaking off and toddlers eating them. Often the same toys can be made from wood, cardboard, or solid types of plastic. Never leave any type of plastic bags or other flimsy types of plastic within reach of young children.

Note: Although the instructions for toys in this book have been written with "kid-proofed" tests in mind, no one can guarantee the absolute safety of these toys or procedures. Use care and common sense to make all toys as safe as possible. Most of the toys described in this book are intended to be made by adults for children to use. Constructing the toys frequently requires the use of sharp tools, such as scissors and knives, which are not safe for children to use. If the children help you make the toys, be careful about possible hazards and supervise the handling of tools carefully. Do not leave sharp tools lying around where children can get into them if you are called away during the construction process.

I.
Infants,
Toddlers,
and
Preschoolers

Sensory Floor Pad for Infants

☀ Say-Along ☀

Babies love soft things to touch:
A furry muff or a powder puff
Are things they like so much.

Babies love hard things to chew:
A large plastic ring, can be just the thing
And baby will figure out what to do.

Babies love some things that make noise:
Rattles to shake, tinkly sounds to make
Can be the perfect toys.

Everything in the world so real
Is fun for Baby to touch and feel.

Who: Nonmobile infants

How to Use It
Place the pad in a strategic area on the floor where the **infant** will be safe from other children and traffic. Place the infant on the pad, facing away from the hustle and bustle of the room and toward the pad's discovery items. This will help the infant concentrate on exploring the items. If, however, the infant seems more interested in experiencing the social activities of the surrounding environment, simply turn her or the pad around.

Introduce the infant to just one of the objects at first by attaching it to the soft Velcro on the pad. When the infant loses interest in the first object, add another that has different qualities from the first. What items seem to excite the infant? What items seem to calm the infant?

Change the items on the pad to suit the infant's developing needs. For example, place large, safe, and clean items on the pad when it seems everything is going into the infant's mouth. Add noisemaking items if the infant shows an interest in making and listening to different sounds.

What It Does
The pad serves as a safe place for the nonmobile infant by creating a clear boundary that the older children can learn to recognize and respect.

The pad also allows you to customize learning experiences to each infant's needs at any given stage of sensory development. And it allows for controlling the sensory stimulus to the optimal level for each child, avoiding overstimulation and frustration.

The pad encourages nonmobile infants to safely explore the materials by touching, smelling, tasting, hearing, and seeing.

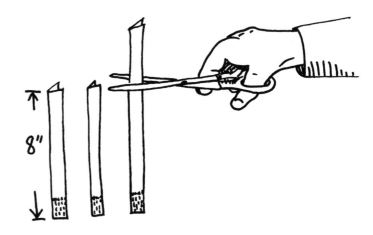

What You Need
- nonallergenic twin-sized mattress pad
- scissors
- wide seam-binding tape or iron-on hemming tape
- needle and thread or iron
- ruler
- Velcro
- glue
- sensory materials that have interesting surfaces, sounds, or smells

How to Make It

1. Fold the mattress pad in half and cut it along the fold to create two sensory pads. You may want to leave the pad in tact and use the folded section for extra padding. Cut other pads to whatever size is desired.

2. Sew seam-binding tape all around (or use iron-on tape) to cover any raw edges.

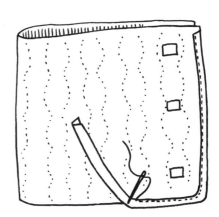

3. Cut three or more 1-inch pieces of Velcro. Glue or sew the soft sides of the Velcro to the top of the mattress pad at strategic locations. For example, three in a row (about 6 to 8 inches apart) on one, two, three, or all four sides of the pad.

4. Cut three or more 8-inch pieces of seam-binding tape. Sew or glue the remaining rough-sided pieces of Velcro to one end of each length of seam-binding tape.

5. Tie or glue one sensory object to the other end of each length of seam-binding tape. Consider using colorful plastic lids, rattles, plastic bracelets, scouring pads, pom-poms, furry material, sturdy play animals, or other toys.

Hanging Mobiles

☀ Say-Along ☀

Twisting, turning, shining bright
_____ loves to watch the light. (*fill in child's name*)
Open wide those little eyes
And see another new surprise.
_____'s eyes move left to right (*fill in child's name*)
As he watches with delight.

Who: Infants

How to Use It

Hang the mobile within sight of the infant. Consider hanging it from a curtain rod, ceiling fixture, clothes hanger, wooden dowel, or tree branch. (The mobile should be out of reach of the child.) The mobile will move gently with the air currents and attract the infant's curiosity.

Create and hang the mobiles with the infant's point of view in mind, making sure that the broad surfaces of the hanging objects can be seen.

Change the hanging objects from time to time. Infants are most attracted to bold, bright colors and contrasting patterns.

Caution: If you have curious toddlers or other young children who may try to investigate the mobile, hang it away from objects that the children can climb (such as tables, chairs, windowsills, and dressers) and use only nontoxic objects that are too large to choke on.

Make sure all hanging objects are securely fastened to the mobile—give each a good shake or tug to be certain.

Remove mobiles or other sensory stimulus any time an infant seems stressed by the extra sensory input or needs to sleep.

What It Does

Bright objects and points of light attract the infant's attention to the objects and encourage focusing, eye movement, and general visual development.

What You Need

- aluminum pie tin
- juice can
- hammer and nail
- button
- yarn, string, fishing line, wire, cord, or shoelaces of various materials
- scissors
- colorful household objects

How to Make It

1. With a hammer and nail, punch four small holes along the rim of the pie tin (equal distance from one another) and one hole in the middle. (Place the area to be punched over the open end of an empty can.)

2. Flatten any rough edges of the holes with the hammer. To hang the mobile, use yarn to tie a knot around the button. Thread the yarn through the middle hole of the tin and make a loop at the other end.

3. Tie yarn to each of the four remaining holes in the tin. Hang objects from the yarn. Make sure the objects balance each other. You can hang any item by itself or in whatever balanced combination you feel will interest the infant. Consider using feathers, plastic fruit and vegetables, plastic utensils, balls, pictures and designs from old greeting cards or magazines mounted on cardboard, empty spools, puffed out Mylar bags, and small plastic bottles.

Variation

A single aluminum pie tin with multiple holes punched on its surface makes a neat light reflector when hung vertically by a sunny window.

Kick Toys for Infants

☀ Say-Along ☀

Watch your feet go kick, kick, kick,
See the toy go flick, flick, flick.
Little feet move quick, quick, quick,
Oh what fun to kick, kick, kick.

Who: Infants

How to Use It

Use elastic to attach this stuffed toy to the side railings of a crib and within kicking range of the **infant**. As soon as the infant shows signs of moving around in the crib, remove the elastic from the toy and the crib so that it becomes a cuddly toy for the infant.

To vary the infant's experience, hang objects that create different sounds or are colorful and visually interesting.

What It Does

The infant is attracted to the toy's facial features and bright colors. Kicking at the toy encourages muscle development and an awareness of cause and effect.

As a cuddle toy, it provides the infant with comfort through the sense of touch and a sense of security from the familiar.

The variations (see below) engage the child's awareness of sounds and movement.

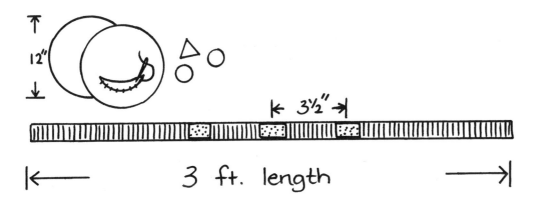

What You Need

- sturdy elastic (2 inches wide)
- ruler
- scissors
- Velcro
- 2 pieces polyester felt or other washable material (about 12 x 12 inches)
- small amount of contrasting material
- needle and thread
- nontoxic paint
- polyester fiberfill or clean panty hose

How to Make It

1. Cut a 3-foot length of elastic. Attach three sections of Velcro across the middle of the elastic strip, approximately 3½ inches apart. Attach the elastic to the side railings of a crib or other convenient play space for infants.

2. To make the kick toy, cut out two circles of the felt or other material, each about 1 foot in diameter. For the facial features, use nontoxic paint or cut out facial features from the contrasting material and sew them securely to one of the felt circles.

3. Add Velcro to the back of the other circle 3½ inches apart (to match the Velcro on the elastic strip).

4. Sew the circles together, leaving a 3-inch opening. Stuff with fiberfill or other material until fluffy. Sew closed.

Variations

Attach noisemaking objects (such as rattles, small wind chimes, or bells) by securely fastening them to a short length of seam-binding tape. Place a small amount of Velcro to the other end of the seam-binding tape.

For added visual interest, attach objects to a short length of seam-binding tape, as described above. Consider using clean and lightly stuffed colorful Mylar-type bags from potato chips, small aluminum potpie pans, or other colorful kitchen objects.

Infant/Toddler Activity Books

☀ Say-Along ☀

Take a look
In this book
And see what you can see.

Soft and furry
Do not hurry
Touch each page with me.

Put things in the special pocket
Here's a baby, try to rock it
Books tell what things can be.

Who: Infants and toddlers

How to Use It

Make these books suit the child's current major interest. Immobile **infants** are most interested in learning the characteristics of materials, so a book for them should include sensory materials, such as colorful pieces of fabric with different textures (including crinkly, smooth, rough, and bouncy).

As children move into **toddlerhood**, they begin to explore and experiment. Add pages that have pockets containing small surprises, such as different colored bracelets, keys, and large key rings. Securely attach objects to the inside of the pocket with short pieces of rickrack or shoelaces. All items must be nontoxic, washable, and too large for a child to choke on or swallow—a minimum of 1½ inches in diameter.

As children begin to recognize objects, books can take on more representational themes, such as a farm featuring animals cut out of furry fabric remnants. Glue one or two figures to each page, labeling each with fabric paint.

Initially allow **infants** and **toddlers** to explore these books in any way they choose. As their interest in the contents grows, sit with them on your lap and discuss the contents with them or "read" the pictures to them. Add appropriate vocalizations for the pictured objects (for example, what the animal says or sounds the object makes).

What It Does

These activity books provide infants with a fun and safe introduction to books, encouraging them to manipulate the pages and look at and feel various textures. Toddlers use them to help satisfy their need to explore and experiment. The books help both infants and toddlers begin to conceptualize the notion that books contain interesting information that satisfies their needs. As children manipulate the pages and find items in the pockets, they strengthen their hand-eye coordination and small-motor skills. "Reading" these books with the infant or toddler enhances the children's receptive and expressive language.

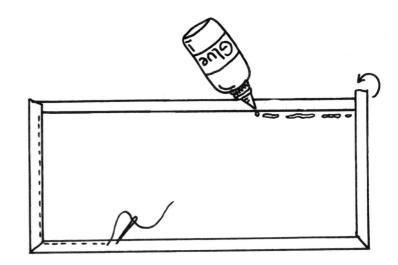

What You Need

- 1 piece of fabric, vinyl, or other material for the cover (about 7 x 15 inches)
- nontoxic washable fabric paint (optional)
- 5 pieces of heavyweight pellon (about 6 x 14 inches) plus some extra for the pockets
- ruler
- scissors
- fabric glue, needle and thread, or sewing machine
- variety of textured fabrics and other materials (such as netting or scrubbing pads)
- small objects
- rickrack, shoelaces, yarn, or cording

How to Make It

1. Decorate the front cover, if desired, with fabric paint or bits of fabric.

2. On a work surface, lay the cover material wrong-side up. Center one of the pellon pieces on top. Fold the excess half-inch of cover fabric over the pellon and around the edges, mitering corners. Glue or sew in place.

3. For pages that do not contain a pocket, glue or sew page contents, as desired, on four pieces (eight pages) of pellon. Center onto inside of cover. Sew or glue each page down the center. Fold in half.

Variation

For toddler books, fashion different kinds of pockets. Sew or glue the pockets in place, one on each page. Cut pieces of rickrack a little longer than each pocket. Sew the ends of rickrack to the bottom inside of each pocket. Tie or sew the other end to an object, such as plastic bracelets, keys, key rings, or flat toys. Hide the object in its pocket.

Cause and Effect Match Board

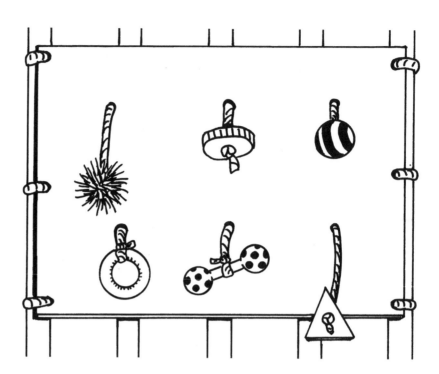

Give a little pull,
Give a little tug,
Now a little tickle,
And a great big hug.
Watch the smile on that
Cute little mug!

Who: Infants and toddlers

How to Use It

When a child pulls an object on the board, the matching object at the other end of the string is pulled toward the board. Tie the board securely to the side of a crib or heavy piece of furniture within easy reach of **infants** or **toddlers**.

At first **infants** may be mostly interested in exploring the objects by grasping, mouthing, and visually exploring the objects. With experience, they will discover that they can activate one object by pulling on the other. Share in the delight of discovery and movement by joining the child in some side-by-side play on the board.

What It Does

The bright colors and different designs on the matching board encourage infants to use their eyes. The cause-and-effect action of the toy appeals to children's interest in movement and change, and it encourages them to take part in making change happen. Using this toy helps infants and toddlers become aware of shapes, colors, and likenesses, and it helps develop hand-eye coordination and small-motor skills as the children discover, grasp, and pull.

What You Need

- heavy cardboard (8 x 11 inches)
- contact paper
- scissors
- X-Acto knife
- sturdy string or cord
- pliers
- nail
- assorted items (such as plastic lids; small, colorful containers; bracelets; rattles; curlers; pom-poms; spools; safe items from games with missing parts; film cans; well-cleaned, small, plastic, moisturizer containers; kitty snack containers; or toy animals)

How to Make It

1. Cover one side of the cardboard with plain colored contact paper.
2. To hang the board, use an X-Acto knife to cut three small holes into opposite sides of the cardboard. Thread 12-inch lengths of string through each hole.
3. Cut six larger holes in the cardboard.
4. Cut three pieces of string: two pieces should be 16 inches long, one should be 20 inches long. Lace each string through two holes. (Lace the longest string through holes at opposite ends of the board.)
5. Choose three pairs of small plastic objects. Use a heated nail to make holes in each item (use pliers to hold the nail while you heat it).
6. Tie the objects to the ends of each string.
7. Tie the board securely to a crib or other area where a child will have easy, safe access to it.

Pull and Snap Toy

❋ Say-Along ❋

Look and see
What can it be?
Grab the _____ (*name the object*)
1—2—3
Hold it oh so tenderly
Now let it go!
Where can it be?
Look inside and you will see!

Who: Infants and toddlers

How to Use It

An **infant** or **toddler** reaches inside the can, finds the object at the end of the elastic, grasps it, and pulls on it. When the child lets it go, the object pops back into the can. This surprising action is much like a reverse jack-in-the-box, which encourages the child to further explore the object and the can.

Toddlers might discover that they can remove the lid that the object is connected to and will practice taking it off and putting it on again. They might also fill the can with other objects, turning it into a fill-and-dump toy.

What It Does

Infants learn grasping and pulling skills. Infants and toddlers practice hand-eye coordination. By constantly having the object pop back into the can, children begin to learn to predict and expect a certain outcome from their own actions. That is, they learn through repetition.

What You Need
- a can with a plastic lid
- can opener
- contact paper
- wide elastic
- scissors
- needle and thread
- graspable object

How to Make It

1. Remove metal ends from a can. Use a can opener to make sure the ends are completely smooth.

2. Cover the can with contact paper, making the contact paper about 1 inch longer than the can at each end. Fold the excess amount over and into the inside of the can.

3. Cut a piece of elastic the same length as the can. Then cut two slits in the middle of the plastic lid, large enough for the elastic to go through.

4. From the inside of the lid, lace one end of the elastic through the slits, and sew securely.

5. Securely fasten the other end of the elastic to the graspable object (such as a pom-pom, small animal, or a soft ball).

6. Place the lid on the can so the object and elastic are inside the can.

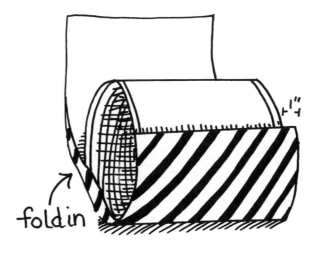

fold in

Box Blocks, Climbers, and Sliders

How to Use It

You can use this set of basic blocks hooked together as a simple space divider for **older infants**. They can pull themselves up with them, place their toys on them, and because the children can still see and be seen over the blocks, they can feel as if they are part of "the group" and yet remain safe behind a boundary of boxes.

Blocks made into a variety of sizes and shapes provide active **toddlers** with many opportunities for movement (climb over, through, around, slide down, and so on). Encourage **older toddlers** and **preschoolers** to use the blocks as an addition to the building-block area. Since you can make these blocks larger and heavier than most blocks, encourage children to work together to pull, push, and lift them into place. Describe to the children what they are doing by saying, "Johnny, I saw you and Ruthie work really hard together to move the red block over by the slide."

Involve **toddlers** and **preschoolers** as you make the boxes. They will love crumpling the newspapers and stuffing them into the boxes.

What It Does

These blocks help to safely confine older infants in a way in which they can still see and be seen. Tailor the boxes to the children. Choose boxes that are the best height for the infants to use for pulling themselves up (large-motor activity), and choose boxes with a flat surface for playing with small toys (small-motor activity). Allow them to be part of the group (social/emotional development).

As a climber/slider module, the boxes develop large-motor skills, muscle strength, and kinesthetic awareness in toddlers. They expand the preschooler's opportunity for more elaborate dramatic play in the block area and for working cooperatively.

When you describe to the children what they are doing, you expand their understanding of language, increasing both their receptive and expressive language skills. This also encourages the cooperative behavior to continue or be repeated.

❋ Say-Along ❋

Look at all that we have done
Building with boxes is really fun,
We've made climbers and a place to slide
And a boxcar train that we can ride.

We crumple up paper every day
To make them strong enough for play,
We stuff them full and tape them shut
Then use them for who knows what.

We can push 'em and pull 'em from here
   to there
Use them to play with most anywhere,
We can even use them like a chair
At a beauty shop while we do our hair.

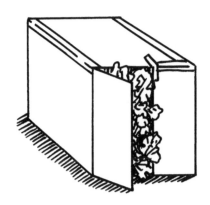

What You Need
- large sturdy cardboard boxes in various shapes
- newspaper
- duct tape or packing tape
- utility knife
- ruler
- pencil

How to Make It

1. Select boxes to suit your needs. Large, flat boxes can be used to make platforms. A number of boxes that are all the same size and shape are ideal for using as building blocks or creating portable barriers. Large sturdy boxes are great for making tunnels, and large rectangular boxes can be made into slides.

2. To weight boxes, tightly stuff them with crumpled newspaper. Tape shut.

3. To make a crawl-through tunnel, push two equal-sized boxes into each other. Cut two holes large enough for toddlers to crawl through, one each on opposite sides. As an option, place a sit-upon in the bottom of the box (see page 70).

4. To make a slide, securely tape all ends of a large box and cut as shown. Stuff bottom part with newspapers. Turn top part around and reposition over bottom to create the slide. For the two pieces to fit together, you may find it necessary to bend down the bottom ramp. Securely tape the two sections together.

Variations
Cover boxes with colorful contact paper or vinyl.

Place Velcro on the boxes to help hook them together when desired, such as for climber/slide combination or a train.

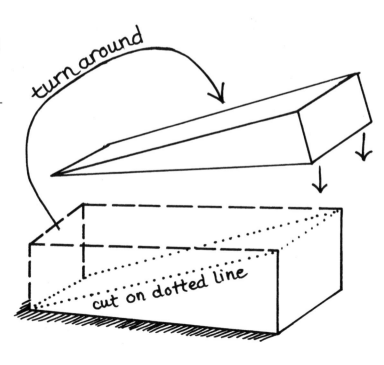

turn around

cut on dotted line

Lid'er Box

Who: Older Infants and toddlers

How to Use It

For **older infants**, remove the plastic lid and let them dump out the metal lids. You can also replace the lid on the can and let them drop the metal lids through the slot, one at a time. **Infants** and **younger toddlers** love the noise the metal lids make. Create several sets of cans and lids so **toddlers** can each have one as they play side by side.

For added interest, mount fabric or pictures of single objects to the insides of the metal lids. **Toddlers** can look for certain pictures or feel the various textures. Encourage **older toddlers** to find pictures or textures that are alike.

What It Does

This toy provides practice in filling and dumping, a favorite activity of older infants and toddlers because of their fascination with objects disappearing and reappearing. Filling and dumping helps in their experimentation with the concept of "object permanence" (learning that things exist even when they can't see them). The activity also helps develop eye-hand coordination and provides sensory stimulation. Language development is encouraged when you talk with the children about the activity and name the pictures, colors, or textures.

What You Need
- large can with a plastic lid
- can opener
- contact paper
- scissors or X-Acto knife
- small pictures or fabric samples
- glue
- metal lids from juice cans

☀ Say-Along ☀

This is one of my favorite toys
I like it 'cuz I like noise,
Shake the can, then dump it out
Now poke the lids in through the slot,
When it's full, shake it some more
Then dump the lids onto the floor,
Fill and dump, dump and fill
Will you help me? Yes I will!

How to Make It

1. Use the can opener around the top of the can until the rim is smooth. Cover the can with contact paper, making the contact paper about 1 inch longer at each end than the can. Fold the excess amount over and into the inside of the can.

2. In the plastic lid, cut a slot about a half inch wide and 2 to 3 inches long. (Use a metal lid as a guide for correct length.)

3. Cut out simple pictures or samples of different textured fabrics and glue them onto the recessed side of the juice can lids. For matching activities, make two of each picture or texture.

Poke and Peek

☀ Say-Along ☀

Into the hole goes the little straw
Now look, it isn't there at all!
Do you wonder where it can be?
Lift the colander and you will see.
Now we'll start again to hide and seek
As we play this game of poke and peek.

Who: Older toddlers

How to Use It

Provide one colander for each group of two to four children. Give each child an envelope containing ten thin drinking straws or plastic coffee stirrers. Invert the colander and encourage the **toddlers** to poke the straws all the way through the holes. Talk about what they are doing and wonder together about where the straws are going. When the straws are all used up, lift up the colander, redistribute the straws, and start over again. After a few times, the children will be able to do this independently. Talk about the importance of only poking the straws into the colander or playdough, never at each other.

What It Does

This appealing activity provides practice in small-motor development and hand-eye coordination. It also provides practice with things disappearing and reappearing—something of great interest, fascination, and importance to toddlers. This is a great side-by-side activity that the children can do together without having to take turns or wait. It offers many opportunities for manipulation and language development. It also is an absorbing individual activity.

What You Need
- colander or a large clump of playdough
- thin plastic drinking straws (cut in half) or plastic coffee stirrers
- envelopes or other small containers
- scissors

How to Make It
1. Place 10 to 15 straws into each envelope or small container. Store the envelopes or containers in the colander for easy access.
2. Give each child one envelope or container of straws. Invert the colander and let the children poke their straws through the holes.

Variation
Let the children poke the straws into clumps of soft playdough.

Parasheet

❋ Say-Along ❋

For preschoolers:

This sheet works like a parachute
We love it 'cuz it's so cute,
Wave it to go up and down
We hide underneath as it falls to
    the ground.

It's neat to wiggle it in the air
And we toss things in it everywhere,
Our teddy bears just love to fly
As we toss them way up toward the sky.

For infants:

This parasheet floats on the air
Sometimes it lands and touches our hair
As we giggle and gleefully shout
While music keeps us bouncing about.

Who: Older infants, toddlers, and preschoolers

How to Use It

Make the parachute the appropriate size for the number of children (and adults) in the group, be it just two, three, or as many as fifteen. Introduce the parachute to **infants** and **toddlers** by having them first sit around it, helping or just watching as the adults lift the edges and wave it gently up and down.

As this activity becomes familiar to the children, they will enjoy finding new ways to use the parachute, such as crawling under it, anticipating its up and down motions, using it to play peek-a-boo with familiar adults, and bouncing to the rhythm of verses or music that accompany the activity.

Older toddlers and **preschoolers** may still enjoy being under the parachute but will especially enjoy using it to toss teddy bears (possibly counting the jumps), bounce a variety of balls, or cooperatively "drive" a small car from side to side.

Encourage the children to think of other things they can do with their parachute. Discuss how air and surface area keep the parachute from falling straight down and how people use parachutes to jump out of airplanes and float down to the ground.

What It Does

The parachute helps infants and toddlers become comfortable with brief separations from trusted adults and experience space differently. It provides practice with the concept of things disappearing and reappearing, as in peek-a-boo. This fascinates older infants and young toddlers who are learning about object permanence. It gives toddlers and younger preschoolers an opportunity to act upon a different material and experience the result of their action. Older preschoolers will experience the concept of catapulting an object into the air using a tool such as the parachute.

Talking about real uses of parachutes develops vocabulary and enhances language development. Counting the times the children can keep a toy bouncing on the parachute provides practice in using numbers.

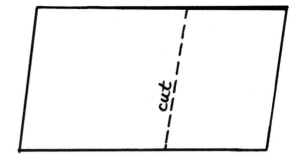

What You Need

- an old flat bed sheet
- ruler
- chalk
- scissors
- sewing machine or iron-on hemming tape
- colorful scraps of material or iron-on designs for decorating (optional)
- small objects to use with the parachute

How to Make It

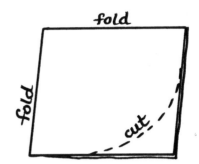

1. Fold the sheet into a square (measure the shortest side, then measure off an equal distance on the long sides). King- or queen-sized sheets are good to use for large groups; half of a twin-sized sheet for groups of two to four participants. Cut off excess material. Fold the remaining square in half, then in half again. Measure the length from the center corner along the folded edge to the end. Using this distance, mark with chalk every few inches to create a semicircle line from edge to edge. Cut along the chalk marks.

2. Create a hem. Decorate as desired.

Variation

Sew small bells inside cloth patches and attach to the top of the parachute to create an auditory element to this activity. If using bells, be sure they are securely attached and covered to prevent infants or toddlers from accidentally choking on them.

The Super Crawl-Over Box

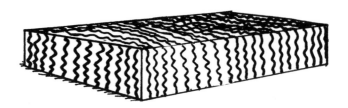

Who: Infants, toddlers, and preschoolers

How to Use It

For **infants,** place the box on the floor. They will enjoy crawling over it or pushing it along the floor. **Toddlers** will find it challenging to lift and carry the box from place to place, balance on it, and jump off it. They might even use it as a stool to help them reach something. You and the **preschoolers** may use it as a stair-stepper for exercising.

What It Does

The box provides a safe way for infants to experiment with new crawling skills, learn to coordinate different large-motor skills, and enjoy the satisfaction of mastering a new skill.

It also allows toddlers to experiment with more difficult large-motor skills such as balancing on both feet, balancing on one foot, stepping on and off, and working on climbing and jumping skills. Toddlers also learn to problem solve, exercise their upper body muscles, and continue to develop large-motor coordination.

What You Need

- sturdy cardboard box (about 3 x 12 x 18 inches)
- newspapers
- tape
- scissors
- colorful contact paper

How to Make It

1. Tightly stuff the box with crumpled newspapers. Tape it shut.
2. Cover the entire box with contact paper.

❋ Say-Along ❋

For infants:

Creeping, crawling, up you go!
Now carefully, go down just so.
Up, Up, Up, Down, Down, Down
Creeping, crawling all around.

For toddlers and preschoolers:

Climb right up and look around (*stand on tiptoes on box, hand shielding eyes*)
Now jump down and touch the ground (*jump off and touch the floor with fingers*)
Here are some tricks for you to try: (*step back up onto box*)
Bend down low, then stretch up high
Balance like an acrobat (*try standing on one foot on the box*)
Now down on all fours just like a cat (*bend down and place hands and feet on box*)
Marching, marching all around (*march around the box*)
One step, two step, up and down (*repeat "up and down" actions*)

Variations

Attach rope handles to one or two sides for easy dragging or lifting.

Make milk carton blocks (see page 188), and tape them together before covering with contact paper to make crawl-over boxes of different sizes and shapes.

Make small stairs for advanced crawlers and toddlers. Create stairs by taping two shallow boxes together, the smaller one centered on the larger one, to create a 6-inch-wide step on all sides. Use sturdy, well-stuffed boxes. Tape them closed before covering.

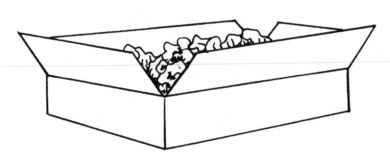

Push-It/Sort-It

Who: Infants, toddlers, and preschoolers

How to Use It

Infants enjoy feeling and visually exploring these soft blocks, dropping them from a high chair, and searching for them in the open can. **Toddlers** will be challenged by pushing the blocks and shapes through the hole in the lid, then dumping them out. They may also enjoy collecting and dumping the blocks into and out of purses or other containers. The soft blocks are perfect for **toddlers'** first throwing practice. Discuss the different textures, colors, and shapes with **toddlers** and **preschoolers. Preschoolers** might use the blocks for throwing and aiming at targets, such as a box or laundry basket, and for playing catch with other people. They can use them as supplements to or instead of other blocks for building.

What It Does

Push-through and stacking activities help hand-eye coordination and small-motor development. Grasping, stacking, and throwing develop large-motor coordination and encourage large- and small-muscle development. Using blocks with others promotes social skills. Matching three-dimensional objects to the one-dimensional openings in the lid promotes problem-solving skills and is a reading-readiness activity.

The blocks and other objects provide opportunities for language development through discussions about colors, shapes, and textures with adults and older children.

What You Need
- nonflammable foam rubber (about 2 inches thick)
- serrated bread knife
- different textured fabrics
- needle and thread
- colorful socks or clean panty hose
- large tin can and several plastic lids
- colorful contact paper
- scissors
- pencil
- tracing paper

❋ Say-Along ❋

This soft and furry little square
Is fun to play with anywhere,
Sometimes I drop it from my chair
And kick or toss it in the air.

Lots of blocks make a tower so tall
Then I push it over and watch it fall,
I can use them like a ball
Even though they're not round at all.

I can squish them and make them small
And push them through holes until they
    fall,
Sometimes they're just fun to touch
'Cuz I like soft things very much.

(Create additional verses to describe the various ways children use these blocks.)

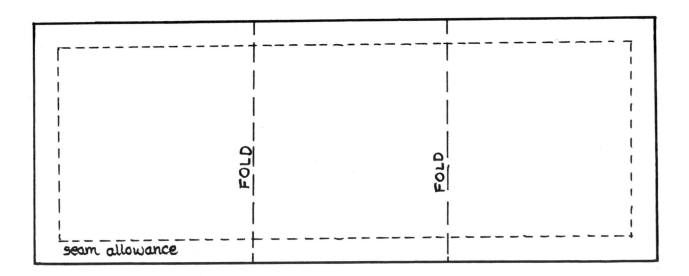

FOLD

FOLD

seam allowance

How to Make It

1. For foam rubber cubes and shapes, use the serrated knife to cut the foam rubber into 2-inch cubes (or different sizes and shapes).

2. Trace a pattern on paper and cut it out. Use the pattern to cut designs from selected fabrics.

3. Cover the foam rubber with fabric (such as corduroy, velveteen, fake fur, or satin) and stitch the seams. Or slip the foam rubber cube into a section cut from a sock or panty hose. Make sure the section of sock or panty hose is long enough to allow for tying off each end with strong thread.

4. Cover the tin can with the contact paper. In the middle of the lid, cut out a square or cut out holes shaped to match selected foam rubber shapes. The greater the child's dexterity, the smaller the holes. For the very young and inexperienced child, make the holes somewhat larger than the objects.

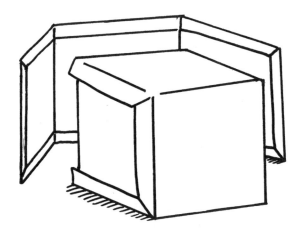

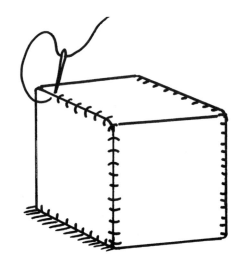

Lacing Things

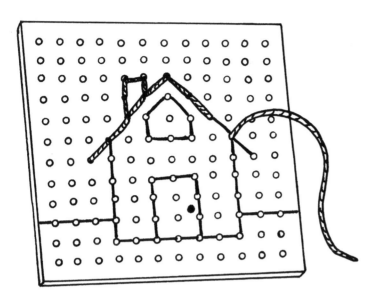

☀ Say-Along ☀

Look at all the things I can lace:
A cat, a dog, and a smiley face,
It's a lot like sewing and not very hard
Just keep on going around the card,
Poke the lace and pull it through
Then go back and forth as I do.

Who: Toddlers

How to Use It

Put out lacing boards and laces for children to use. Older children may want to make their own lacing cards by tracing pictures on plastic lids or Styrofoam trays and punching holes along the outline of the picture.

For easier lacing, use leather or plastic-coated laces and tie a knot at one end. Pull the lace through one hole near the picture's corner to get started and demonstrate poking the lace through the holes along the outline, going back and forth from the front to the back of board. Younger children may lace in random fashion and not follow the outline.

Talk about the pictures or the lacing frames, naming various parts of the pictures. Also, discuss the concepts and words involved in the lacing process, such as *front, back, over, under, inside, outside, outline,* and *edge.*

What It Does

This activity provides desirable, sturdy lacing boards that will last much longer than cardboard sewing cards. Lacing encourages hand-eye coordination, small-motor development, and problem-solving skills. Talking about pictures and concepts expands vocabularies and encourages language development. Older children who make their own lacing cards are provided with an opportunity to plan and execute a project from beginning to end. This promotes creativity, encourages refinement of small-motor skills, and enhances children's self-esteem.

What You Need

- material for the lacing board (such as a 9-inch square section of pegboard, plastic lid, or Styrofoam tray)
- pattern from coloring book pictures, large patterned contact paper
- pencil
- permanent markers or paint
- scissors
- glue
- hole punch
- cloth tape
- lacing materials (such as shoelaces, rug yarn, or leather)

How to Make It

1. Draw pictures of common objects or cut out pictures from coloring books or contact paper.

2. For pegboard lacing boards, trace the pattern onto the pegboard with a pencil. Fill in the picture with permanent marker or paint.

   For plastic lid lacing cards, attach the picture to the lid. Punch holes around the outer edge of the picture or around the edge of the lid. If possible, cut the rim off the plastic lid so a hole punch can reach the outline. Tape around the edge.

3. Cut the lacing material into lengths of 15 to 18 inches. If you are using yarn, coat the ends with glue to stiffen them and prevent fraying.

Variation

Assemble a variety of household items children can use for lacing, such as colanders, slotted spoons, or spatulas. Toddlers will especially enjoy lacing these items.

Bucket Brigade

☀ Say-Along ☀

This is my bucket
See how I lug it
I carry it all around.

Pop off the top
Let the things drop
And scatter all over the ground.

Back in they go
I put them just so
Through the slots that I found.

Who: Toddlers

How to Use It

Toddlers can dump objects out of the plastic bucket and try to fit them through holes in the lid. The smaller items will fit through any of the holes, but the larger ones require some searching and experimentation before the **toddler** will find a hole that will work. You may need to help in removing or replacing the lid.

Repeat the dump-and-fill process as long as the **toddler** remains interested, providing assistance as needed. Resist the temptation to find the right hole for the toddler. Simply provide encouragement when the toddler needs it. Toddlers also enjoy carrying the bucket around and adding other toys to the collection. Talk with the toddlers about what they are doing and the characteristics of the objects they are fitting into the holes.

What It Does

This activity provides the toddler with a portable and enjoyable dump-and-fill toy. It encourages hand-eye coordination, small-muscle development, and problem-solving skills. Young toddlers are fascinated with fill-and-dump toys because of their need to explore and understand the idea of things existing when they can't see them. With your guidance, the disappearance and reappearance of the objects encourages language development, reasoning, and making associations.

What You Need

- large, clean, plastic bucket with lid
- assorted objects (such as soft curlers, film cans, small face cream containers, kitty treat containers, plastic cookie cutters, small blocks)
- X-Acto knife or scissors
- markers

How to Make It

1. Remove the lid from the bucket. On the lid, trace around each object you have collected.

2. Using a knife or scissors, follow the tracings to cut holes in the lid. Test to make sure each object fits through its hole. Place objects into the bucket and replace the lid.

II.
Older
Toddlers
and
Preschoolers

Simple Lotto

❋ Say-Along ❋

Oh do you know
How to play lotto?
It's quite an easy game.

You pick a card
Then look real hard
To find one that looks the same.

You cover each spot
With the cards you've got
Till you finish up the game.

Who: Older toddlers and preschoolers

How to Use It

Older Toddler and **preschoolers** match pictures to a duplicate glued to the master playing board. Children can play alone or in a group.

To play lotto, place individual cards face down in a pile. Give each player a master playing board. Have children take turns picking cards and searching for the matching picture. Let the child who picks the card be the main searcher, but encourage all the children to help find it. Continue playing until all cards are covered. Do not stress the idea of being first to have a board covered. Instead, emphasize the group process and keep everyone involved.

What It Does

Lotto teaches recognition of likenesses and differences. Matching pictures or patterns helps children learn visual discrimination, which is a pre-reading skill. The game also provides opportunities for taking turns and for cooperative game playing.

Put three or four pictures on the master playing boards to create a simple game for younger children (ages 2 to 3). For older children, make master playing boards with six pictures on them.

What You Need

- pictures
- 8 unlined index cards (8 x 5 inches) or tagboard
- scissors
- glue
- ruler
- black marker
- clear contact paper

How to Make It

1. Cut out matching sets of different pictures, such as gift wrapping paper, contact paper, or wallpaper. One set is for the master playing boards, and the other set is for the matching cards. For younger children, you will need 24 pictures to make four sets (three pictures on each card). For older children, you will need 48 pictures to make four master playing boards (six pictures on each board).

2. Draw lines on the each index card to form six boxes (draw three or four boxes for younger children).

3. Create two index cards with identical pictures on them by gluing one of each matching picture to separate index cards. Cover with clear contact paper.

4. Leave one set of cards uncut to use as the master playing boards. Cut the second set along the lines to create the playing cards.

Magnet Match-Ups

☀ Say-Along ☀

Do you know what we call designs on
   our clothes?
If it has many colors, it's a pattern that
   shows,
Patterns come in all different styles
Using lines or dots or even smiles.

Some lines are straight and some are
   squiggly
Some patterns show shapes looking
   wiggly,
The thing about patterns that I didn't
   know:
They keep on repeating themselves
   just so.

That's what makes it a pattern that looks
   the same
Whether plaid or polka dot is its name.

**Who: Older toddlers and
preschoolers**

How to Use It
There are many different ways
children can play with these lids.
Toddlers will enjoy using them to
fill and dump from a container.
They also will enjoy putting them
on and taking them off a metal surface (such as a refrigerator door or a
cookie sheet).

Encourage **older toddlers** and **preschoolers** to match
the patterns that look alike and then put them next to each
other on the refrigerator door (or other metal surface). Talk
about the patterns and what they look like. Use words such
as *plaid, striped, geometric design, floral print,* and *polka dot.* Also
discuss any textures the fabrics may have, such as furry,
smooth, silky, or bumpy.

Have the children try matching the textured fabrics with
their eyes closed. Discuss the concepts of same and different
and all the words and concepts associated with the patterns,
fabrics, or pictures, as well as concepts related to magnets.

Older preschoolers can use the lids to play concentration games or make up other sorting games. For example,
they may separate all the similar patterns (all plaids, all floral
patterns) into baskets.

What It Does
These lids encourage children to pay attention to the detail
involved in matching like items, which uses both visual- and
tactile-perception skills. They provide an introduction to the
workings of magnets and an opportunity to emphasize some
basic language concepts, such as pairs, patterns, and textures.
All of these help expand children's vocabularies and language
comprehension. Manipulating the lids and fill-and-dump
activities help toddlers develop their small-motor skills and
hand-eye coordination.

What You Need
- juice can lids
- scissors
- file cards (optional)
- magnetic tape
- tube container
- pattern and texture samples
- glue stick
- colorful contact paper (optional)

How to Make It
1. Cut circles from the pattern and texture samples (two of each pattern or texture) to fit inside juice can lids. Consider using fabric scraps, wallpaper samples, or wrapping paper patterns.
2. Glue a circle onto each lid. (If a sample is very delicate, first mount it on an index card, then cut it into a circle to fit the lid.)
3. Place a small piece of magnetic tape on the reverse side of each lid. Store the lids in a tube-like container. If desired, cover the tube with contact paper.

Do-Able
Read books to children that introduce and discuss the idea of patterns and pairs. An excellent one from the Math Start Series is *A Pair of Socks,* by Stuart J. Murphy (Harper Collins, 1996).

Other books on this topic are *Dots, Spots, Speckles, and Stripes,* by Tana Hoban (Greenwillow, 1987) and *Patterns,* by Henry Pluckrose (Children's Press, 1995).

For another do-able related to magnets, see "Magnet Mysteries" on page 122.

Flexible Feely Board

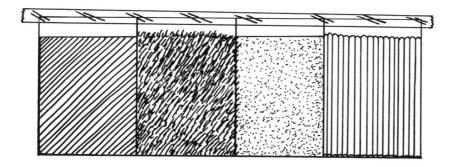

Who: Older toddlers and young preschoolers

How to Use It

Find a variety of contrasting textures to attach to the feely board. Display the board at the children's eye level so the **toddlers** can touch it and visually explore it. After the **toddlers** have explored it on their own for a period of time, extend the learning process by describing to the children what they are feeling and seeing. For example, as a child touches a piece of sheepskin with wool on it, say, "Soft. The wool is soft." When the child touches a piece of sandpaper, say, "Rough. The sandpaper feels rough."

Encourage **young preschoolers** to test their language skills by playing a game that asks them to put on a blindfold, feel a texture on the board, and then guess what it is or describe what it feels like. For both age groups, make a variety of boards that can be changed as desired.

What It Does

This activity helps toddlers learn the characteristics of materials through their sense of touch and sight (an ongoing method of learning). When you describe the sensation for the toddlers, they begin to associate the sensations with the descriptive words. Older toddlers and young preschoolers are able to practice the use of descriptive language as they describe or guess what they are feeling. This activity also helps extend toddlers' vocabularies and the knowledge of basic concepts associated with touch and textures.

What You Need
- tagboard
- texture samples
- scissors
- ruler
- glue
- Velcro or tape
- wide headband
- shoe box for storage

❋ Say-Along ❋

To play this game we don't need much
Just our hands to use to touch,
We'll let our fingers run and play
Feeling all the things along the way.

Some things are soft and some are furry
But the rough ones make my fingers
    hurry,
Over to something I like much better
That feels just like my favorite sweater.

And what I learned from playing this
    game:
Lamb's wool is this fabric's name.

How to Make It

1. To make a feely board to which you can affix various textures, cut the tagboard into pieces about 5 x 7 inches. (You also can use the back of writing tablets or panty hose inserts to make the base of a feely board.)

2. Cut each piece of sensory material 1 inch shorter than the board. Consider using pieces of vinyl, satin, sandpaper, scrubbing pads, fur, netting, foam, or wool. Glue a different sensory material onto each board, leaving a 1-inch space at the top of the board uncovered. This space can be used to mount the feely board to a surface (such as the refrigerator, a door, the side of bookshelf, or a wall).

3. For older toddlers and three year olds, have a wide headband available to cover their eyes for when they want to play the "feel and guess" game. Store the feely boards in the shoe box.

Variatons

For a more permanent feely board, glue different textures onto a large piece of tagboard, leaving a 1-inch uncovered edge along all sides of the tagboard. Tape the board to the selected surface.

Use the "Child-Safe Display Rack" (see page 184) for mounting the feely boards.

For older children, convert the feely boards to a matching game. Attach a strip of Velcro next to each texture. Cut small samples of the same textures that are used on the feely boards and place a strip of Velcro on the back of each one. Keep the small samples nearby in a container. Children can place the small samples next to matching textures on the board.

Feel and Tell Box

Who: Older toddlers and preschoolers

How to Use It

Toddlers will enjoy playing with the texture samples. **Preschoolers** can play the matching game. For the game, a child reaches into the box with one hand and feels one of the texture samples. Before removing the sample, the child tries to find its match by touching the texture pieces mounted on the lid. When a texture on the lid is chosen, the child removes the piece from the box to see if the two are the same. Encourage the child to repeat the process until matches are found for all the pieces.

Talk with the child about the different textures as well as the concepts of same, different, matching, and pairs. Repeating the say-along verse provides a fun way to learn how to play the game. This game can be played by one child alone or several children at a time.

❋ Say-Along ❋

Put your hand in the box
To see what you find!
Now study the top
To find the same kind.

Check it out! Are they the same?
Good! That's the way we play this game
   (if the match is correct)
Try again, as we play this game.
   (if a mismatch)

What It Does

This activity encourages the child to identify items by touch as well as sight. It helps develop awareness of different textures and the many words used to describe them, such as *rough, smooth, bumpy, soft,* and *furry.* The activity also provides practice in using the words and concepts crucial to understanding the idea of matching and finding pairs.

What You Need
- shoe box with lid
- texture samples
- scissors
- cardboard or tagboard
- glue

How to Make It

1. Cut two squares of each texture sample. Consider using steel wool, sandpaper, fabric scraps, and paper.

2. Glue a sample of each texture onto the lid of the shoe box.

3. Glue the remaining texture samples onto squares of cardboard or tagboard. Place them inside the shoe box.

4. In one end of the shoe box, cut a hole large enough for a child's hand. Put on the lid.

Variation

Make a game that matches objects to pictures of the objects. Mount pictures of objects on a different shoe box lid. (You can use the same shoe box from the activity described above.) Put the matching objects inside the shoe box. Objects to use include a small ball, key, comb, block, car, crayon, and a spoon.

Where's the Scoop?

How to Use It

Older toddlers and **preschoolers** match cutouts of scoops of ice cream to the cone of the same color. Encourage the children to tell you what color they are matching or point to or tell you other things that are the same color. Discuss what flavors various colors might be and what flavors the children like best.

❄ Say-Along ❄

What color scoop did you find?
Pink for strawberry, my favorite kind,
Now look at all the rest
How many like chocolate best?

Its color is kind of brown
What other colors have you found?
For many, vanilla is just right
To find its scoop, look for one that's
    white.

It's fun to look at colors and see
What flavors they could possibly be,
But some colors just won't do
What flavor do you think is blue?

What It Does

This activity teaches color matching and recognition to two to three year olds. Finding the correct scoop shapes and putting them in outlines above the cone shapes encourages hand-eye coordination.

   The variation (see below) encourages children's number awareness and helps build number recognition skills. Add extra scoops to the game so that children can match quantities to numbers (for example, three scoops are put on the cone with a number three on it).

   Discussion about ice-cream cones and flavors encourages the use of imagination and vocabulary development.

What You Need
- construction paper in eight colors
- cone and scoop patterns (see below)
- pencil
- scissors
- file folder
- glue
- black marker
- clear contact paper
- paper clip
- small plastic bag

How to Make It

1. Trace the pattern of the cone and scoop onto construction paper, making one set from each color. Cut out the patterns.

2. Glue the cone shapes onto the file folder. Draw a cross-hatch design on them. Draw the outline of a scoop above each cone.

3. Cover the file folder with clear contact paper.

4. Cover both sides of the scoop shapes with clear contact paper. Place them in a small plastic bag for storage. Clip the bag to the edge of the file folder.

Variation

Use this activity as a number matching game. Use wipe-off crayons or washable markers to number each cone from one to eight. Place a corresponding number of stickers or small dots on one side of each scoop.

For an easy number match, keep the color of the stickers or small dots consistent with the color of the cone and scoop. For a more difficult game, vary the marker color.

If you add the dots or stickers *after* the clear contact paper has been placed over the cones and scoops, you can alter them and change the sets or combinations.

Scoop

Cone

Shoe Box Train

☀ Say-Along ☀

This train is busy all day long
And while it works it sings this song:
"Choo, Choo, Chug, Chug,
Choo, Choo, Choo,
Carrying things is what I do." (*repeat last three lines*)

Who: Older toddlers and preschoolers

How to Use It

Older toddlers will use this homemade train as a pull toy. They also will enjoy putting their toys and stuffed animals into the boxes and using the train for fill-and-dump games. Encourage **older toddlers** to take the toys for a ride, and talk about what they are doing.

Let **older toddlers** help decorate boxes, and encourage them to watch as you assemble the boxes into a train. **Preschoolers** can make their own trains and use them to dramatize stories such as "The Little Engine that Could." They can also set up a railroad yard and station in the dramatic-play area.

What It Does

This train provides toddlers and preschoolers with a chance to help create a toy they can use in play. They may imitate the process with other boxes. The train gives them ideas for imaginative play. Talking about trains and how people use them stimulates language development. Read stories about trains and encourage children to use the train to retell the story.

What You Need

- shoe boxes of various sizes
- markers
- paper circles
- glue
- scissors
- yarn or string
- drinking straws
- large button

How to Make It

1. Let the children use the markers to decorate the boxes. Glue on the paper wheels. (If you want the wheels to turn, use cardboard circles and attach them with brass fasteners.)

2. Poke holes at both ends of each shoe box. Make only one hole in the box that will be the caboose.

3. Connect the boxes with pieces of yarn or string. Run the yarn or string between the cars through drinking straws to create links that will not become slack. Knot yarn securely inside each box.

4. Attach an 18-inch-long piece of yarn to the front car and tie a large button onto the end of it to use as a handle.

Water-Play Kit

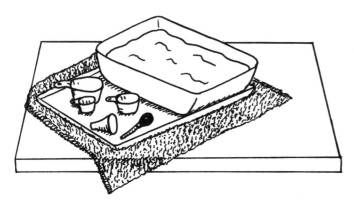

☀ Say-Along ☀

Water is so much fun to play
I could play with it every day,
I'll fill up all these cups to pour
And when that's done, I'll do some more.

I love to feel water on my hands
I love to pour and watch it as it lands,
Look at all the jars I fill
And then tip over and watch them spill.

Don't ask me why kids love water so
I'm sure no one will ever know,
But maybe water's great appeal
Comes from its wonderfully soothing feel.

Who: Older toddlers and preschoolers

How to Use It

For indoor fun, fill a dishpan or small basin one-third full of tepid water. Place the dishpan and an assortment of pouring toys on a jelly roll pan. The jelly roll pan will catch spills and help keep the play in a defined space. Place a bath towel or small rug under the jelly roll pan to help absorb spills and to keep the jelly roll pan stationary.

One to two children should use each dishpan or basin. Set up additional stations for more children.

Encourage **older toddlers** and **preschoolers** to use the cups for pouring and to experiment with the basters, funnels, and tubing. Demonstrate how to use basters or eyedroppers to draw up water and how to cover the tops of tubes with a finger to pick up water and drop it again. If necessary, show children how funnels help when pouring water into narrow openings such as toy baby bottles. See the variations (below) for additional water-play kits to use for washing clothes or dishes and for sinking and floating experiments.

What It Does

Playing with water is an exceedingly satisfying and soothing activity for young children. Water is a material they can easily control. Being able to pour it into different kinds of containers provides endless fascination. While water play is usually enjoyed as a sensory experience, it also engages children to learn about measurement, quantity, and the nature of comparing amounts of liquid. All of these contribute to their later understanding of the logical-mathematical concept that a half cup of water is the same amount of water in any shape container (an idea younger children do not grasp but water play helps them learn).

Water play also encourages experimentation, which helps demonstrate some of the scientific principles involved in sinking, floating, displacement, uses of pressure, and laws of flow—all of which fascinates children.

What You Need
- water-play items
- plastic dishpan
- water
- jelly roll pan
- container to hold water items

How to Make It

1. Put water-play items on the jelly roll pan. Consider using measuring cups, spoons, large plastic lids, funnels, basters, eyedroppers, sieves, strainers, small pieces of plastic tubing, and small plastic jars. Make sure the items are clean.

2. Fill the dishpan one-fourth to one-third full of tepid water. Place the dishpan on the jelly roll pan along with the water-play toys. Place the pan and toys on a towel or rug, if desired.

Note: With proper supervision, you easily can use water play indoors as well as out. The younger the child, the smaller the amount of water you should use to begin with. Also use small amounts of water with an older child who has had only bathtub experiences with water.

Variations

Assemble additional water-play kits for a variety of activities. Consider the following:

Washing Clothes or Dishes: small packet of soap (Ivory Flakes, Ivory Snow, or Dreft), eggbeater to mix suds, container and plastic pitcher for rinse water, clothes or dishes to wash, bath towel to lay washed items on or clothespins to hang clothes.

Sink or Float: small items (sponges, corks, rocks, Styrofoam items, small boats, wood pieces, metal spoons), two storage containers (one for objects that float and one for objects that sink).

Color Mixing: small plastic jars, eyedroppers, plastic spoons, food color or a few drops of tempera paint (optional: items to dye, such as large pasta, eggs or eggshells, scraps of paper).

Squish Bags

☀ Say-Along ☀

Squeeze and squish
Pull and push
This is just like making mush.
Slide your fingers on the top
Like making waves that never stop.
Watch the colors change with ease
As you give the bag a squeeze.
Squish bags can be lots of fun
Would you like to play with one?

Who: Older toddlers and preschoolers

How to Use It

Let the children squeeze and manipulate the bag to feel the texture of the material inside the bag and blend the colors together. Add more food coloring to darken or change the colors. Talk with the children about what they are experiencing as they work with their squish bags. Use the bags for as long as children are interested in manipulating them.

Children can also use the squish bags to mix frosting for decorating cookies. To squeeze out the frosting, snip a small section off one of the corners. Let the children decorate the cookies as they wish.

Caution: This activity requires close supervision.

What It Does

Squish bags provide fun sensory explorations for toddlers and preschoolers. Children can observe how colors are mixed together to create yet another color. The activity enhances language development as well as small-motor skills. It can also provide a clean introduction to fingerpainting for children who are reluctant to do so.

What You Need

- small- or medium-sized heavy-duty plastic bags
- smooth-textured products (shaving cream, whipping cream, pudding, whipped frosting, mustard, ketchup)
- food coloring
- cookie sheet

How to Make It

1. Put a smooth, white product (such as shaving cream) into a bag. Use smaller bags for manipulation, color mixing, and frosting. Use larger bags for fingerpainting.
2. Squirt in several drops of food coloring (use just one color).
3. Add more of the smooth, white product so the food coloring is surrounded.
4. Gently squeeze as much air as possible from the bag and seal it shut. Let children manipulate the bag. If desired, open the bag and add a second color or a second product. Reseal as before.

Twist and Turn

Who: Toddlers and preschoolers

How to Use It

Introduce this activity by demonstrating each phase as described in the verse. Place containers that hold jars and lids on a table or the floor. Children can unscrew the tops from the jars and mix them up, then find the ones that fit and screw them back together again. One child can do this alone, or two children can work together, taking turns picking a top and trying to find the correct match. At the end of the game, ask the children to screw the lids on the jars so the lids don't get lost.

What It Does

As they screw and unscrew the lids, children practice hand-eye coordination, visual discrimination, and small-motor skills. This activity helps establish the association of one lid to each jar and encourages associations of size to match lid and jar. This activity fascinates two-and-a-half to three-year-old children.

What You Need

- container (such as a plastic bowl with a lid or a shoe box)
- eight to ten assorted small plastic jars with screw-on lids
- 3- x 5-inch index card
- marker
- tape
- clear contact paper

How to Make It

1. Clean and dry the jars and lids. Be sure each lid fits only one jar. Consider using jars from cosmetic products, spices, baking or food items, baby products, suntan lotion, and sample or travel-sized jars of shampoo and lotions.

2. Place the assortment of jars and lids in a container.

3. Create a label for the container by drawing a picture of jars and lids on the index card. Tape the label to the container in a prominent place and cover with clear contact paper.

☀ Say-Along ☀

Look inside this box and find
A game of a most unusual kind,
It isn't advertised on TV
But it's lots of fun as we will see.

These jars are all for us to use
Just twist the top and it unscrews.
Take all the jars and lids apart
When that's all done then we'll start.

We twist and turn each lid to see
Which jar it fits most perfectly,
Then put together every one
Till all the jars in this box are done.

Keys for Learning

☀ Say-Along ☀

Do you like to play with keys?
Here, I'll give you a set of these.
Take them to that board and look
Each key has its own special hook.

Some have round tops, some are square
The outline card will show you where,
To find the hook for every one
Playing with keys is lots of fun.

Who: Older toddlers and preschoolers

How to Use It

Children place keys on hooks, trying to find keys that match the picture outline on each hook. Prop the board with all of the hooks in it against a wall or on a chair, then select a set of key outline cards and keys. First put the outline cards on the hooks, then encourage the children to study the keys carefully, noticing the shape of the top and bottom of the key.

Younger children will enjoy simply putting the key on the hooks and ignore matching the shape. They could, however, match keys of different colors to colored outlines. Encourage older children to match the wiggly line side of the outline to the actual key.

To make the game easier, use quite differently shaped keys in a set. To make it more difficult, use similar keys and make the outline of each key very precise.

What It Does

Putting keys on hooks develops hand-eye coordination and small-motor skills. Children love to play with keys, and this gives them an interesting thing to do with them. Matching the key shapes provides a difficult and challenging perceptual task for older preschoolers.

What You Need

- 8- x 10-inch plywood board
- sharp tool or small drill to start holes
- ruler
- L-shaped screw-in hooks (about $1/16$ inch size)
- pliers (optional)
- index cards (4 x 6 inches) or tagboard per set
- old keys of various sizes and shapes
- fine-tipped color markers
- scissors
- clear contact paper
- hole punch
- large plastic or metal key rings or large paper clips

How to Make It

1. Use a sharp tool or drill to start making the holes in the plywood. Use pegboard and hooks as an alternative. Make two rows of three small holes. Leave about 2½ inches between each of the holes, and approximately 4 inches between rows. Twist the hooks into the holes. A pair of pliers will make the task easier. Be sure the hooks do not go through the back of the plywood.

2. Cut index cards or tagboard into 2- x 3-inch pieces. Trace around a different key on each card. Make a dot in the key hole. Cover cards with clear contact paper.

3. Punch holes on the dot of each key outline card. Place keys and matching cards on a large ring or paper clip. If you are making multiple sets, you may want to color code the cards and keys that go together.

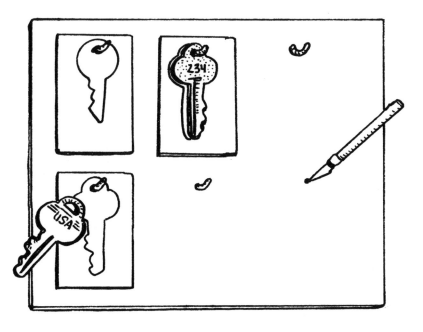

Things to String

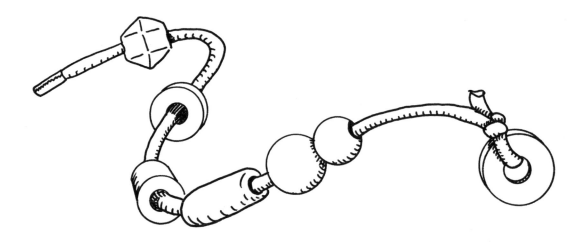

Who: Older toddlers and preschoolers

☀ Say-Along ☀

What can you do with that round
   rubber thing?
Slip it on the tube just like a string!
Now take another, try some more,
Count how many: 1, 2, 3, 4.

These are really fun to string
But what shall we call this long thing?
It can be a necklace or a crown
Or maybe some cars sliding up and
   down.

When all your stringing fun is through
Then unstring the tube is what to do,
Be sure to put all the things away
So you can string them another day.

How to Use It
Set out containers of plastic tubes and large rubber washers
(make several sets so children can work together). Allow the
children to figure out what to do with the materials or teach
them how by example. It is easy for toddlers to string washers on tubing because the tubing stays erect. Add different
stringing materials to challenge the **preschoolers.**

What It Does
This activity makes the first attempts at bead stringing more
successful for toddlers by avoiding the frustration caused by
standard laces. Stringing enhances hand-eye coordination and
control of small muscles. Enhance sensory development by
using the tubing and washers in water play.

Preschoolers will practice pre-reading and pre-counting
skills as they match and count a variety of stringable items,
and they will also fine-tune their hand-eye coordination.
Discussion of the different-sized items enhances language
development.

What You Need

For toddlers:

- lengths of plastic tubing
- large rubber washers with holes
- scissors
- tape
- spools
- keys with large holes or on key rings

For preschoolers:

- thin tubing, shoelaces, or wrapping cord
- metal washers
- tape
- assorted beads
- various containers

How to Make It

1. Cut tubing or string into sections that are 18- to 24-inches long.
2. Form a stopper by tying one end of each tube or string around a washer. Tubing and washers come in different thicknesses and are available in hardware or plumbing supply stores. If you are using string, tape the other end to make threading easier and prevent fraying.
3. Set out various sizes of washers, buttons, and beads. Preschoolers can help sort the items into containers for storage.

Variation

Use rubber washers and tubes in the water table. Children can blow bubbles through tubing and string the washers onto the tubes.

Caution: To avoid the spread of disease, provide each child with a tube and sanitize the tubes after each use. Be certain that the beads and washers are too large to swallow. This activity requires close supervision.

Clothespin Capers

☀ Say-Along ☀

Clothespins can be lots of fun
Watch me as I slip them on,
Over the end, around the side
See how they slip and slide?
You know what else I sometimes do?
Find some holes to poke them through!

Who: Older toddlers and preschoolers

How to Use It

Toddlers will enjoy placing slip-on or clip-on clothespins onto the rims of containers, such as plastic cottage cheese containers or small boxes. They may also push them through holes cut in the lid of a container. Encourage **older toddlers** and **preschoolers** alike to use the clothespins in imaginative play. Draw faces on the clothespins. Cut holes in the lid that are too small for the clothespins to slip through. The children may then line up the clothespins on the lid as athletic teams or space people. **Preschoolers** can play matching games by matching colors, numbers, letters, names, dots, stars, or tiny pictures attached to the container and the clothespins.

What It Does

This toy gives toddlers opportunities to fill and dump and refine hand-eye and coordination skills. Toddlers may also use the clothespins in imaginative ways, from stirring something in a pot to pretending they are people parading about. Preschoolers will develop small-muscle control and strength; gain color, number, and symbol recognition skills; and develop language and imaginative play skills.

What You Need

- slip-on or clip-on clothespins (depending on the ages of children)
- containers with lids
- scissors
- markers
- a variety of colored tape
- stickers

How to Make It

For toddlers:

1. Cut one or more holes in each of the lids. Consider using cottage cheese cartons, milk cartons cut in half, or small boxes.
2. Make some holes big enough to allow the clothespins to slip through and some that are smaller so that they hold the clothespins. Draw faces on the clothespins, if desired.

For preschoolers:

1. Depending on the skill level of the children, either follow the directions above or the directions for creating matching games (below).
2. Place matching colored tape, numbers, or symbols on both the clip-on clothespins and the container.

Styrofoam Pounding Bench

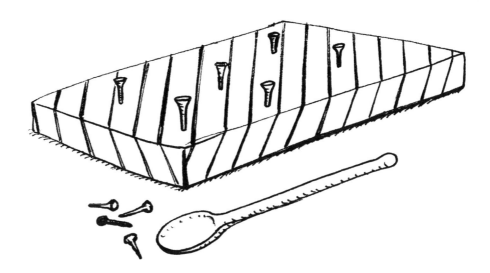

☀ Say-Along ☀

First it was a crate around our TV
Now look at what it's going to be,
A pounding bench to use with golf tees
To pound and hammer as much as we
please.

We'll use it to hammer until it's through
Then turn it into sculptures for me
and you,
We're using it for lots of play
While recycling it along the way.

Who: Older toddlers and preschoolers

How to Use It

Put out large, heavy-duty sections of Styrofoam used for packing appliances, televisions, and other electronics. Also set out containers of colorful golf tees and mallets (such as wooden spoons or small hammers from pounding toys). Encourage the children to practice pounding golf tees into the sections of Styrofoam. The children can pound in the tees as far as they like, but they should remove and return them to the storage containers when they are finished. Encourage **older preschoolers** to count how many tees they pounded as they remove them from the sections of Styrofoam. Older children can also make designs using the colorful tees and yarn, ribbon, flags, or tissue paper.

When the Styrofoam can no longer be used as a bench, break it into pieces. Older children can create sculptures by connecting the Styrofoam pieces with straws, toothpicks, old pens and other colorful materials. Be sure to keep the small pieces away from infants and young toddlers who might put them in their mouths.

What It Does

This bench creates a useable pounding toy from a throwaway item, which demonstrates a way of recycling materials. Pounding helps children develop hand-eye coordination and small-motor skills.

Making up designs or sculptures encourages the use of imagination and creativity and contributes to artistic development and appreciation.

What You Need

- large, heavy-duty Styrofoam packing pieces
- X-Acto knife or small saw
- golf tees and container
- contact paper
- bowl or resealable plastic bag
- two small mallets or wooden spoons

How to Make It

1. Cut the Styrofoam into sections about 1½ x 2 feet. Cover the section with contact paper to reduce shredding and make cleanup easier.

2. Collect golf tees and put them into the container. Set them out with the Styrofoam bench and the mallets (small hammers or wooden spoons, for example).

Variation

When the Styrofoam is beginning to come apart from all the pounding, place pieces from the broken-up bench or Styrofoam packing noodles into a plastic bucket. (To cut down on static cling, lightly spray the Styrofoam and bucket with a solution of water and a small amount of fabric softener.) Collect items to use as connectors (such as coffee stirrers, straws, toothpicks, old pens, round colored toothpicks, or baggie ties). Place the connectors in a plastic bag and add it to the bucket.

Encourage older children to make designs or sculptures using decorative materials, such as colorful yarn, ribbons, flags, and tissue paper scraps.

Take-Apart Teddy

❈ Say-Along ❈

This teddy bear is really neat
'Cuz you can remove his hands and feet,
And put them back where they belong
Or mix them up and do it wrong.

Since that makes the bear look so funny
You can even give him ears from the
    bunny,
Inventing new animals can be lots of fun
But take care of the pieces when you're
    done.

Who: Older toddlers and preschoolers

How to Use It
Older toddlers and **young preschoolers** enjoy taking apart these animal figures, sticking them back together again, and putting decorative bows or clothes on them. Encourage **older toddlers** to touch and talk about the textures and parts of the animal. Play mix-and-match games with the torsos, limbs, and features. Keep the animal parts, bows, and clothing together in a large plastic container or wicker basket for easy access.

What It Does
The animal figures encourage small-motor development and thinking skills through take-apart and put-together activities. The toys provide tactile and sensory stimulation and call attention to the body parts of the animals, how they fit together, and their names.

Discussing the parts of different animals helps build vocabularies and encourages children to compare likenesses and differences as related to shapes and sizes. Exchanging parts of the animal figures and creating a new animal can encourage the development of humor.

What You Need
- large, brown piece of felt
- small, colored pieces of felt
- pencil
- scissors
- fabric marker
- Velcro
- fake fur or fabric scraps
- needle and thread (optional)

How to Make It

1. Make copy of the bear pattern (page 56) and trace the pieces onto brown felt.

2. Cut out the felt pieces. With the fabric marker, draw a face on the head.

3. Cut small pieces of Velcro and sew them to the front of the body and to the back of the body parts, as shown on the pattern.

4. Trace the bow pattern on a small piece of colored felt or decorative fabric and cut it out. Attach Velcro to the back of the bow. Make several different colored bows.

5. Cut several circles from the fake fur or fabric scraps to use as clothes. Make the circles approximately the same size as the part of the animal figure it will cover. Attach Velcro pieces to the back of the clothes.

Variations

Make patterns for other animals. Use drawings from coloring books or picture books for inspiration.

For three and four year olds, use buttons or snaps in addition to Velcro to help teach the small-motor skills needed to work these fasteners.

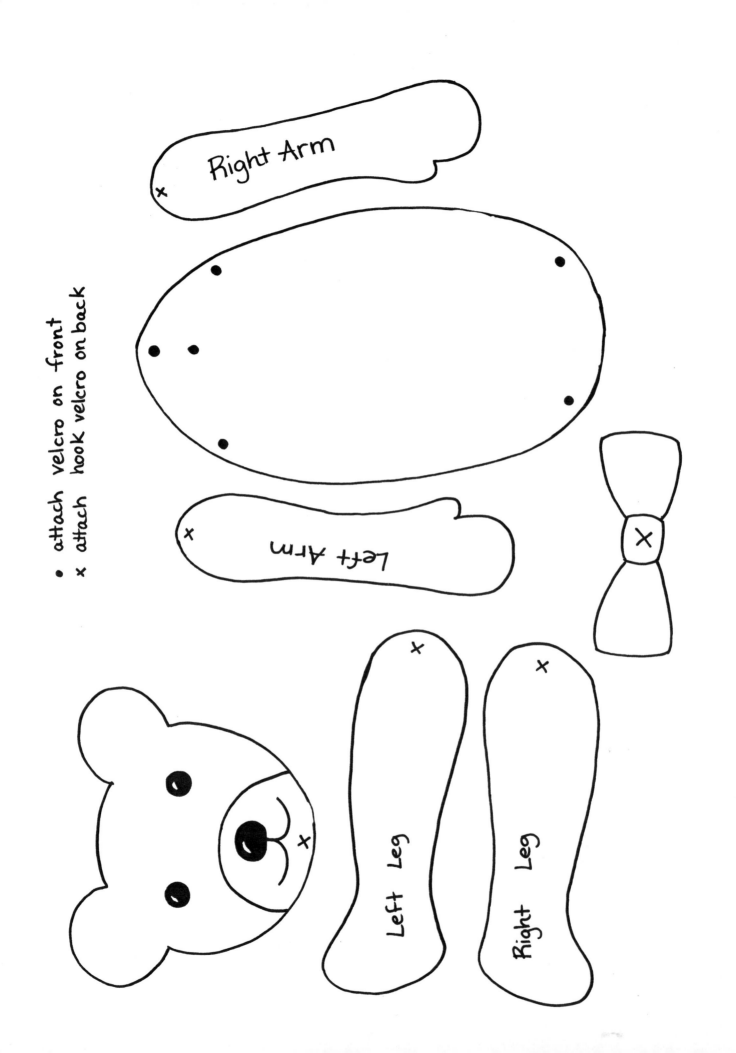

III.
Toddlers, Preschoolers, and Schoolagers

Picture Puzzle

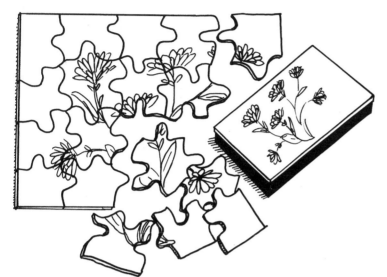

☀ Say-Along ☀

Working a puzzle is so much fun
We put the pieces together until it's done,
But if you want puzzles to be easy for you
Here are some things that you should do.

First look at the puzzle so you can see
What the picture ought to be,
Next take out each piece one by one
'Cuz it shows you how the puzzle's done.

Ready to go—now let's begin
You can fit the pieces in,
Look at the picture for a clue
The shape of the piece can also help you.

Find the spot where each piece will fit
You might have to turn them a little bit,
When working puzzles just think it
   through
And they will always be fun to do.

Who: Toddlers, preschoolers, and schoolagers

How to Use It
Encourage the children to fit the puzzle pieces together. Encourage **older preschoolers** and **schoolagers** to help make the puzzles. You and the children can describe the colors and shapes of the pieces as they assemble the puzzles. Discuss the objects that are pictured in the completed puzzle. Make up stories to fit the pictures.

What It Does
Puzzles encourage problem-solving skills and learning how parts fit together to make a whole. They also help children learn to be aware of shapes, colors, sorting, and matching (all pre-reading skills). Puzzles help to develop hand-eye coordination. Talking about puzzles encourages language and social skills. Letting the children help in the process of creating the puzzles encourages their creativity and enhances their self-esteem.

What You Need
- magazines with colorful photographs and pictures
- tagboard or cardboard
- scissors
- glue
- clear contact paper
- flat box and cover or a large envelope

How to Make It
1. Cut out a magazine picture. Glue it onto the tagboard or cardboard and cover it with clear contact paper.

2. Cut the magazine picture into puzzle pieces. Cut large, simple pieces for toddlers. As the age and abilities of the children using the puzzles increase, cut more and smaller pieces.

3. Draw or glue a likeness of the puzzle on the box lid or envelope. Store the puzzle inside the box or envelope.

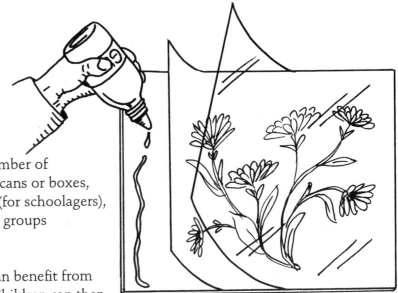

Variations

Puzzles can be made from an unlimited number of
materials. Consider using labels from food cans or boxes,
kids' drawings, traced pictures, road maps (for schoolagers),
and enlarged photographs of individuals or groups
of children.

To help toddlers and other children who can benefit from
it, create various borders for the puzzles. Children can then
use the borders to help them put the puzzles together. There
are three possible ways of making borders for the puzzles:

- To create a border around the outside of the
  puzzle, use two pieces of cardboard, both
  pieces being 1 to 2 inches larger than the picture. Center and glue the picture onto one of
  the cardboard pieces. Cut out the picture. Glue
  the frame that remains to the other piece of
  uncut cardboard. Cut the picture into puzzle
  pieces. Children can then put the puzzle
  together inside the border without the frustration of the pieces slipping around.

- With a felt-tip marker, trace the puzzle shapes
  onto the bottom of a flat box or sanitized
  Styrofoam meat tray. The tracing marks
  will show how the pieces fit together.

- Trace the outline of the puzzle onto the bottom of a flat
  box or sanitized Styrofoam meat tray that is larger than the
  puzzle. Glue a heavy piece of yarn or cord onto the outline
  of the puzzle. Allow the glue to dry completely. Children
  can then put the puzzle together inside the yarn boundary
  without the frustration of the pieces slipping around.

Felt Boards to Go

☀ Say-Along ☀

This special board is so much fun
'Cuz the pictures stick to it one by one,
Here are the three bears
Sitting in their chairs,
And the three little kittens
Holding up their mittens.

What I really think I'll do
Is make up stories to tell to you,
I'll make up one about Winnie-the-Pooh
Taking care of Baby Roo,
They're searching for a honey pot
Which he put away and then forgot.

Perhaps I can make up some more
About a purple dinosaur,
Or a bunch of trains with funny faces
That keep on going to wonderful places,
Oh yes, I can even repeat
Stories from that famous street.

Who: Toddlers, preschoolers, and schoolagers

How to Use It

This activity uses a felt board in both traditional and unique ways. For example, use cutout characters and a felt board to retell favorite stories, or use the felt board as a counting activity that matches objects to numerals. Spell names and words with felt letters, make up matching or sequencing games, or use figures to discuss body parts, feelings, or actions. Individually, children can make pictures or designs with cutouts or match patterns that are provided on cue cards. As a group activity, provide specific directions to follow (for example, "Put five yellow circles on your board," "See if you can find some shapes that make a house," or "Put a tree next to the house").

To use as matching games, have the children match or copy designs or pictures drawn on master pattern cards. To stimulate discussion of feelings or body awareness, provide felt cutouts of heads, eyes, smiles, frowns, arms, legs, and torsos.

What It Does

Felt boards offer children a variety of manipulative, sensory, and creative experiences. Making pictures fosters creativity and an understanding of design concepts. Counting out objects to match numbers helps teach the meaning of numbers. Playing with letters helps children learn to recognize and become familiar with letters. Retelling stories or matching design patterns helps develop memory skills and an understanding of sequencing and language concepts. All of these various activities help build reading readiness and social skills.

The box top felt boards and the felt board variations (see below) are easy to transport for an extra activity on a field trip or for use outdoors.

What You Need

- box with lid, such as a gift or shirt box (about 10 x 14 inches)
- felt or Velcro to fit the lid
- material for cutouts (such as felt, Velcro, flannel)
- glue
- scissors
- markers
- resealable plastic bags
- labels

How to Make It

1. Glue felt or Velcro to the inside of the box lid.

2. Use the chosen material to make cutouts in shapes, designs, and quantity required. You can also buy precut felt letters and numbers.

3. For retelling favorite stories, trace storybook characters and props onto the chosen material. If you have old storybooks, cut out images of the characters and glue a small piece of Velcro or felt onto the back and use them for retelling stories.

4. Store the pieces for each story in a separate resealable plastic bag and label with the story title and identifying picture. Also store cutouts of shapes, designs, and patterns in individualized bags.

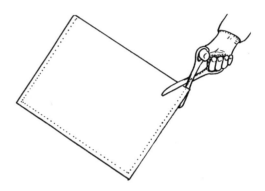

Variations

Make a felt board using bolt ends (the cardboard rectangles around which fabric is wrapped in fabric stores). Staple one end of the felt, flannel, or Velcro to the bolt and roll the felt around the bolt for easy storage.

You can also make a felt board by wrapping felt, flannel, or Velcro around heavy tagboard or cardboard sheets, about 9 x 12 inches. Store the board and cutouts in a large manila envelope.

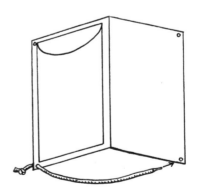

Create an easel-style felt board using a cardboard book mailer. Cut away all of the cardboard from the mailer except the front and back and one long side of the box that creates a hinge.

Cover the entire outside surface with felt, flannel, or Velcro and glue in place.

To each inside part of the cardboard, glue a business-sized envelope or 7- x 10-inch manila envelope so the flap is exposed. The envelopes can be used to store the cutouts.

Poke a hole in each of the four corners of the board when it is laid out flat. Bend the board into a tent shape, felt side out. Thread two lengths of 12-inch long string or shoelace through the front holes and then through the back holes. Tie each end into knots large enough to prevent them from slip-

ping through the holes. This makes a neat two-person, easel-style felt board or an easy store-and-tote flannel board for individual children.

Here is another easy way to create an easel-style felt board: Cut two equal-sized pieces of sturdy cardboard. Create a hinge by taping together the two long sides of the cardboard pieces. Use duct tape to make the hinge strong. To allow for the bend in the hinge, leave approximately a half inch of space between the two cardboard pieces. Cover the entire outside surface with felt, flannel, or Velcro and glue in place. Proceed as in the above variation.

Create pattern cards on index cards or cut-up file folders. Ideas for patterns include shape sequences cards, pictures made from shapes, and designs (such as parquet block designs).

Have children place felt pieces on the board as you tell the following story, or use it as a finger play. Encourage the children to enact the accompanying motions.

A Winter Time Tale
(author unknown)

The chubby little snowman (*swing arms around body in a wide circle*)
Had a carrot nose; (*point to nose*)
Along came bunny (*place forefinger and index finger in V*)
And what do you suppose? (*hop the hand with the ears sticking up*)
That hungry little bunny (*rub hands over stomach*)
Looking for his lunch; (*place hand above eyes, spy fashion*)
Ate that little snowman's nose (*pretend to eat carrot*)
Nibble, nibble, crunch!

Instant Paintbrush

Who: Toddlers, preschoolers, and schoolagers

How to Use It

When you attach clothespins to cut-up sponges, the clothespin becomes the handle of a paintbrush that children can use at a table, easel, or outdoors. Make a variety of different-sized and different-shaped sponges for interesting effects. Let children wash the sponges after each use. Store the paint-brushes in a covered container and keep them on the shelf ready to use.

What It Does

These paintbrushes provide an easy-to-make, easy-to-use, and low-cost alternative to purchased paintbrushes. These brushes make painting less messy by keeping the children's fingers out of the paint, and they encourage even reluctant painters to try. You can turn any object—from feathers to leaves—into a paintbrush. These brushes also encourage creativity and imagination in exploring the use of new ideas and materials, as well as hand-eye coordination in assembling and using the brushes.

What You Need

- sponges or other materials (such as feathers, leaves, pom-poms, cotton balls, or pieces of string)
- scissors
- clip clothespins
- tempera paints and water
- muffin tin or assorted small plastic containers with covers
- paper

How to Make It

1. Cut the sponges into a variety of sizes and shapes. Assemble the other materials you want to use. Clip to the clothespins.
2. Mix tempera paints with water (or use premixed paints) and pour into the containers. Leave two or three containers empty to hold extra brushes.

✹ Say-Along ✹

This little clothespin without any fuss,
Can turn things into a neat paintbrush.
With sponges or strings,
It can paint many things.

See me make a little fish,
Or some ice cream in a dish.
Now I'll turn that into slush,
With my handy little paintbrush.

Picture and Word Books

Who: Toddlers, preschoolers, and schoolagers

☀ Say-Along ☀

Let's make up a story about things we do
To help take care of me and you.
 (*point to each other*)
We'll try to remember to put things
 away, (*pretend to stack toys*)
And to be very careful as we play,
And we'll try to be kind to others today.
We'll write it down in our helping book,
 (*pretend to write*)
So we can always take a look. (*pretend to
 read a book*)
And see how we helped each other, each
 day,
We'll tell it all in our special way
And make sure everyone has something
 to say.

How to Use It

Make books for **toddlers** with pictures of things that are familiar to them. Let the children turn the pages and tell you what they see or ask questions for you to answer. Change the pictures to reflect the changes in their world.

Older toddlers and **young preschoolers** can begin to tell you stories about the pictures. **Older preschoolers** and **schoolagers** can make their own books, either drawing or cutting out pictures and dictating the stories to you. **Schoolagers** can make picture books for the younger children. All children will enjoy a book containing pictures of their family. They can share it with others in the group or find comfort in it on difficult days.

What It Does

Because the pages of these books are made from resealable plastic bags, you can customize them in ways that will reinforce many of the toddlers' new discoveries. The books give toddlers opportunities to practice new words, learn what books are all about, and experience the joy of turning the pages. The books foster an interest in reading in preschoolers and enhance listening skills. Describing pictures, storytelling, and writing their books encourages verbal expression and creativity.

Reading with another person provides a way for the children to learn new words and concepts and gain information about the world. Reading also helps to develop social and communication skills. Writing and creating books is an excellent reading readiness activity.

What You Need

- 4 to 8 resealable plastic bags
- tagboard
- scissors
- glue
- magazines with pictures, snapshots, or drawing materials
- needle and thread or sewing machine
- bias tape or cloth tape (optional)
- stapler
- clear plastic tape

How to Make It

1. Cut a piece of tagboard about ⅛ inch less than the inside measurements of the plastic bags.

2. Glue visual images to each side of the tagboard pieces. Consider collecting these images from magazines and snapshots, or draw them yourself. Leave space on the tagboard pieces for recording stories or labeling.

3. Slip each piece of tagboard into its own plastic bag, with the open end of the bag at the top. Stack the bags with all the openings at the top.

4. Sew the left side of the plastic bags securely together. For optimal strength, cover the binding side with bias tape or cloth tape before sewing. School-agers can make books by stapling the sides together first, then taping over the staples.

5. Change the images and material in the plastic bags to create theme books that will engage the children. Consider the following ideas:

   People Books: Pictures of each child with his or her name written underneath encourage self-esteem and name recognition. Extend this concept by adding pictures of the child's family, home, pets, and friends.

   Feelings Books: Pictures of children showing different emotions help children identify or discuss a particular emotion. Ask questions to prompt discussion (for example, "Are you feeling sad like this boy?" "Are you feeling angry like this child?" "What can we do to help you feel better?").

Feely Books: Attach different textures to the tagboard pieces and insert them into the resealable plastic bags. Cut out a small circle in the middle of each plastic bag. Infants and toddlers can touch the textures and discuss them with you, using descriptive words such as *smooth, rough,* and *fuzzy.*

Theme Books: Anything new or familiar that captures the child's interest and abilities makes for effective theme books. Consider using items like coloring books, counting books, books on the seasons, and various shapes to create theme books. Use the theme books to convey concepts such as self-care or taking care of nature. Or create theme books that focus on finding similarities, such as things that fly, things that talk, or things that swim. This is a great way to create a book that addresses a child's special interest. Trains, cars, dogs, fish—the possibilities are endless!

Action Books: Use each plastic page to store items that can be removed, such as small puzzles, matching games, tricks, lacing cards, or origami instructions and paper.

Stack-a-Lot Containers

Who: Toddlers, preschoolers, and schoolagers

How to Use It

Toddlers may practice putting the containers inside one another and taking them out. They may turn them over and stack the containers into towers or line them up as barriers.
Preschoolers may experiment with rolling the containers. Teachers can model self-talk in the children's presence. For example, "I wonder if this fat can fit into this skinny can?" Then try it and continue to self-talk about the results.
Schoolagers can use the containers to measure and chart the different sizes and arrange the containers in order of diameter, circumference, or height. Write the words *small, smaller, smallest* and *big, bigger, biggest* on cards for the schoolagers to use in their measuring experiments.

What It Does

These containers help children understand size differences, shapes, and word concepts. They encourage exploration, creative building-play, and the development of small-motor skills. They also provide hands-on experiences with physical characteristics, such as round objects roll.

What You Need

- a variety of different-sized empty cans, plastic containers, boxes, or tubes
- colorful contact paper
- scissors
- can opener

How to Make It

1. Clean the containers thoroughly. If using metal cans, use the can opener to go around the rim of each can several times to make sure there are no sharp edges.
2. Cut colorful contact paper 1 inch longer than each can. Cover each can with the contact paper, folding the extra over the rim.

Variation

Instead of using colorful contact paper to decorate the cans, use construction paper, clear contact paper, and pictures cut from magazines. Cut the construction paper to fit the outside of the can and glue in place. Glue pictures onto the construction paper and cover with clear contact paper.

❋ Say-Along ❋

A small can, (*cup hands for a small can*)
A medium can, (*move hands slightly apart*)
A great big can I see. (*move hands far apart*)
Shall we count them?
1, 2, 3 (*use fingers to represent each number*)

Styrofoam Boats and Other Floatables

Who: Toddlers, preschoolers, and schoolagers

How to Use It

Toddlers will enjoy experimenting with Styrofoam and exploring how a simple Styrofoam boat or raft floats. They might try to see how much they can load onto their watercraft before it sinks, or they may use it for transporting other toys.

Preschoolers will begin to incorporate their watercraft into dramatic play, such as pretending that people are fishing from their watercraft. Along with this dramatic play will be a continued exploration of what conditions cause objects to sink or float.

Schoolagers can use these watercraft in their more complex play to dramatize everything from the sinking of the *Titanic* and taking a whitewater rafting vacation to being barge captains on the Mississippi River. Older children can begin to learn vocabulary words associated with watercraft, such as *stern, aft, starboard,* and *anchor knot.*

☀ Say-Along ☀

Do you like my special boat?
Watch and see how it can float
It can be a great big barge,
And since I'm the captain, I'm in charge.
I'll tell the crew to load it with care,
Then take the goods from here to there.
On lakes or rivers it carries heavy loads,
But it would need some wheels to go on
  roads.

What It Does

These watercraft encourage fantasy play and creative expression in all ages. Boats and other floatables give children hands-on experience with the concept of staying afloat and sinking. Older children may be interested in learning about water displacement, which is the concept that the volume of water displaced by a boat must weigh more than the boat to keep the boat from sinking. Children can learn the many ways people use watercraft (such as for recreation and transportation of goods) and the different kinds of watercraft.

To enhance the children's language skills, select and read books to them or talk with them about what they are doing with their watercraft play.

What You Need

- a variety of Styrofoam trays and containers (such as those used for meat, fruit, sandwiches, and eggs)
- assorted trim items (such as spools, cord, pipe cleaners)
- scissors
- waterproof glue
- small-sized, heavy objects (such as flat rocks)
- string

How to Make It

1. Be creative! For the base, choose a Styrofoam container that best suits what you plan to make. Then glue other pieces of Styrofoam containers or other items to the base, outfitting it as you see fit. This is a great project for schoolagers to do on their own.

2. To stabilize the craft, glue a small object in the center bottom of the craft.

3. If you're going to launch the craft outside on puddles or rivulets, tie a string to the craft so the children can guide it.

Backpack and Sit-Upon

☀ Say-Along ☀

Our backpacks and sit-upons are really
   dandy,
On neighborhood walks they sure come
   in handy.
We can sit down almost anywhere,
For a story or a snack to share.

We wear our backpacks to walk around,
Collecting things that we have found.
Now on a "Trash Hunt" we are bound,
To help clean up our own playground.

Who: Preschoolers and schoolagers

How to Use It

Children can use their backpacks for dramatic play and for carrying lightweight objects or treasures found on walks.

The sit-upon makes a waterproof pillow for outdoor dramatic play (such as going camping) or for real use when on a nature hike, watching a sports event, having a picnic, or listening to a story outdoors.

Children can carry their sit-upons in their backpacks for ready availability. The envelopes on the backpack can hold important notes or information, such as each child's emergency referral number. Be sure children's names are on the envelope in case it becomes separated from the pack. The envelopes also allow the children to keep items that they have collected separate and to keep fragile items safe from objects in the larger pack.

Encourage the children to take care of the environment while on walks. Their backpacks can be used to collect litter, such as pop cans, bottles, or trash.

What It Does

These inexpensive and practical props encourage creative play. Wearing the backpack on walks allows and encourages being responsible for one's own possessions. They can enhance real nature experiences as well as encourage classroom discussion and learning about many different kinds of outdoor adventures, such as camping, canoeing, hiking, and climbing mountains.

What You Need

Backpack:

- 1 large grocery bag per child (2 bags per child if you want the backpacks to be extra sturdy)
- 1 manila envelope per child
- 2 business-sized envelopes per child
- glue
- markers and other materials for decorating the outside
- 2 tagboard strips or other suitable material, 1½ x 24 inches, per child
- masking tape or duct tape
- scissors
- stapler
- cards with children's names and emergency phone numbers

Sit-Upon:

- old newspapers, foam pellets, or other light stuffing material
- 2 large heavy-duty resealable plastic bags per child
- sharp pin
- masking tape or duct tape

How to Make It

Backpack

1. If using two bags, fit one inside the other. Fold in 2 or 3 inches of the rim.
2. Glue the manila envelope to the front of the backpack. Make sure to leave one end of the envelopes open. Glue the business-sized envelopes to the sides of the bag. Write the child's name on the envelopes and the backpack.
3. Let the children decorate their backpacks.
4. Staple one end of the tagboard strips near the center of the backpack's top. Staple the other ends near the outside edges at the bottom of the backpack. Reinforce with tape. Make sure the straps fit in a way that allows the child to easily put on and take off the backpack.

Sit-Upon

1. Shred newspapers (children love this part) or prepare other stuffing materials. Put the material into one plastic bag until the bag is plump. Make small holes (pinprick size) in the corners of the bag to release air.
2. Zip the bag shut and slip the other bag over it so the zippers are at opposite ends. Zip the second bag shut. Reinforce with tape for extra durability. Repeat the air removal procedure for the second bag.

Do-Able

Take a walk and clean up your yard or neighborhood. Line the backpacks with plastic grocery bags. Have children walk in pairs so one child can collect trash while the other collects recyclable cans and bottles. Be sure to have children wash their hands after handling trash or have them wear gloves. When cleaning up a neighborhood park or playground, do the collecting on the return walk.

Very Kool Playdough

Who: Toddlers, preschoolers, and schoolagers

How to Use It

All children love to use playdough to roll, knead, pat, shape, cut, poke, and create everything from cookies to creatures. **Toddlers** mash, pat, and roll the dough. For **older toddlers** and **preschoolers**, extend playful uses with props such as round blocks or rolling pins, cookie cutters, molds, muffin tins, and tea strainers. **Schoolagers** can help make the playdough and use it to create imaginative characters and animals.

Make one color of playdough at a time, or make several colors available to create new colors, such as red and yellow to make orange.

See if children can tell what fruit or berry flavor was used by smelling the dough. To make the smell test more challenging for older children, blindfold them first or put the dough in a paper bag so they can't see the color.

What It Does

Making the playdough helps older children learn to measure, mix, read a recipe, and follow directions. Using the playdough enhances the children's creativity, provides practice in using hands and fingers to control and manipulate a material (small-motor skills), and offers a soothing, relaxing sensory experience. Mixing different colored playdough teaches color identification and how to make colors.

This is a great recipe for homemade playdough. It is safe for young children because of its low salt content. It is long lasting and easy to clean up, it is not grainy, and it smells good.

☀ Say-Along ☀

Pat-a-cake, Pat-a-cake
Look what I can make,
Cookies in so many shapes
Lots and lots of long, long snakes.
Roll it into a little ball
Or stretch it into a tree so tall,
Knead it, roll it, poke it too
See what else you can do.

What You Need

- 2½ cups flour
- ½ cup salt
- 1 Tbsp. alum (found in the spice section of most grocery stores)
- 2 envelopes unsweetened drink mix
- 3 Tbsp. cooking oil
- 2 cups boiling water
- covered plastic container or resealable plastic bag

How to Make It

1. In a large bowl, mix together the flour, salt, alum, and drink mix. Add the oil and the boiling water to the dry ingredients. Mix well.
2. When the mixture is cool enough to handle, knead it until it is well mixed, then let it cool.
3. Store the playdough in the refrigerator in the covered container or resealable plastic bag when not in use.

Variation

Use different flavors (and colors) of drink mix to vary the smell and look of the playdough.

Fancy Fish

Who: Toddlers, preschoolers, and schoolagers

How to Use It

Toddlers and **three year olds** will enjoy decorating the premade fish with markers and stickers. Older children can create and decorate their own fish-shaped bags but may need help tying the ends shut.

Before making the fish, show children pictures of fish. Discuss with them where fish live and their body parts, including their bright colors, tail shapes, and eye placement.

Decorate the room with the fish, create a tropical fish display, or use them in dramatic play about fishing, snorkeling, or scuba diving. Attach strip magnets to the fish and have children "fish" for them with a homemade fishing pole.

☀ Say-Along ☀

See the fish
Go swish, swish, swish,
As they swim to the bottom of the sea.
Their colors bright,
Reflect the light,
Oh, please, catch one for me.

What It Does

These fancy fish are a fun craft activity that can teach children about tropical fish and ocean life by illustrating the shape and characteristics of real fish. Use them to create an interesting table display about the ocean, adding other items such as shells, coral, and rocks.

Creating the fish uses small-motor skills, and "fishing" for them requires large-motor development and concentration. The use of fish in dramatic play or displays encourages development of language and imagination. Make lots of fish and let the children think of things to do with them.

What You Need
- small paper bags or shiny Mylar bags from snack packs
- glue stick
- coding dots, stickers
- markers and crayons
- scissors
- newspaper
- yarn
- strip magnet, large metal bolt, and long pole or stick (optional)

How to Make It

1. Lay the bag flat. Fold the closed corners toward the center of the bag and glue them to form a fish shape.

2. Decorate both sides of the bag using markers or crayons. Stick on coding dots for eyes on each side. Optional: Use scissors to fringe the open edge of the bag.

3. Have children shred newspaper and stuff it into the bags. Do not overstuff. Tie the end shut using the yarn 2 inches from the tail end.

4. For a fishing activity, glue a 1-inch piece of strip magnet onto the side of the fish. Tie a metal bolt to one end of a length of yarn, and attach the other end of the yarn to the pole or stick for a homemade fishing pole. (Keep the string very short for young children and beginners. Lengthen the string as their abilities grow.)

Do-Ables

Read books about the sea and the creatures that live in it. *Sea Shapes,* by Suse MacDonald (Voyager, 1998) has beautiful illustrations showing all the interesting shapes and colors in the sea.

Sing or recite songs about the ocean and its wildlife. *Busy Fingers, Growing Minds,* by Rhoda Redleaf (Redleaf Press, 1993) has several verses that fit well with this theme, including "My Gold Fish" and "5 Little Fishes."

Portable Easels

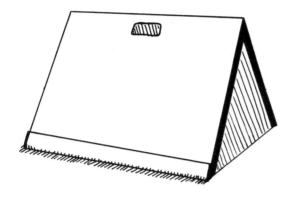

❋ Say-Along ❋

I went outside to look at a tree
And took my easel and paints with me,
I stood under the tree and looked up high
Through the branches I could see the sky.

Then I plopped down on the ground
And with my eyes looked all around,
I took my paintbrush in my hand
And painted a tree that was really grand.

Who: Toddlers, preschoolers, and schoolagers

How to Use It

Have two children share an easel, or make one per child. Place the easels on any surface (indoors or out) that is suitable for the children's height. Allow **toddlers** and **younger preschoolers** to experiment with their brushes and paints.

As their skills develop, **older preschoolers** and **schoolagers** might enjoy painting representations of what they see, each in his or her own way. On a field trip, for example, encourage children to look at the surrounding scenery and paint what they like. Have the children tell you the story of their picture.

Show the children how to take care of their paint and brushes. Encourage them to keep covers on the paint when not in use and thoroughly clean their brushes before storing them in the slots inside the easel. Attach papers to the easel with clothespins or large paper clips. Older children can attach their own paper.

What It Does

You can easily make enough of these inexpensive, easy-to-store easels so a small group of children can be painting at the same time. Having a number of easels on hand is especially important when toddlers are involved because it is difficult for them to wait their turn. These easels facilitate spontaneous use of art materials because children can set up a painting project whenever and wherever they feel like it. The easels also teach children to be resourceful and encourage them to be responsible for their art materials.

What You Need

- large, sturdy, square cardboard box (about 20 inches per side)
- heavy vinyl, oil cloth, or other waterproof material
- utility knife
- pencil
- ruler or yardstick
- stapler or duct tape
- scissors
- clothespins or large paper clips
- Velcro
- six-pack juice cartons for paints

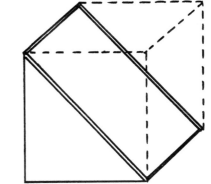

How to Make It

1. Place the box bottom up. Cut apart along one bottom edge, from corner to corner. Draw a line and cut diagonally from cut corner to opposite corner on two sides. Trim off flap from top of box.

   Note: Two easels can be made from one box if the top can be taped shut. Then instead of cutting the flap off, you end up with a second easel.

2. Cut a 2-inch slot out of each side of the top edge of the easel.

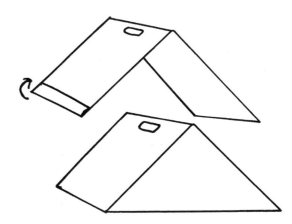

3. For the waterproof covering, measure the width of the easel and the overall length, then cut out a section of oil cloth that is 4 inches larger. Fold up 2 inches of each end and staple or tape along the side (this creates pockets to contain any extra paint drippings). Drape the cloth over the easel and cut out 2-inch slots at the top to match the ones in the cardboard. Clip a clothespin or paper clip in each slot on each side.

4. On the inside of the easel, attach 2- to 4-inch strips of Velcro, side by side, about 2 inches apart. Lay cleaned brushes across the strips and lay the corresponding Velcro strips over the brushes. (See "Scissors and Sundry Tool Holder," page 78, for alternate brush storage.)

5. Cover the outside of the juice cartons with vinyl to reinforce them for carrying paints.

Variation

If using flannel-backed oilcloth, you can turn the easel flannel-side out and use it as a flannelboard.

Scissors and Sundry Tool Holder

Who: Toddlers, preschoolers, and schoolagers

How to Use It

Use this tool holder to safely store and carry scissors or other tools. A large coffee can holds ten or more scissors or paintbrushes. Small cans can hold one to two of each or one pair of scissors and one paintbrush. The smaller cans can become individualized holders, allowing children to be responsible for the tools they use. Encourage children to return scissors and other tools to the slots when not in use, placing them point-side down.

For groups sharing tool holders, use two medium-sized cans and spread out the cans at the worktable for easy use.

What It Does

These tool holders provide a safe way for children to carry and care for scissors and other tools and keep them readily accessible for use. The holders enhance neatness, organizational skills, and responsibility for materials, as well as encourage self-directed activities using scissors. The holders protect scissors and other tools from being dropped or falling off tables and shelves.

What You Need
- coffee can or other can with plastic lid
- contact paper or other decorative covering
- markers
- utility knife

How to Make It

1. Cover the can with the contact paper or another covering. When suitable, let the children help decorate the can.
2. Place the plastic lid on the can. Use the utility knife to make suitable holes for paintbrushes, rulers, and other tools.
3. Place a pair of scissors into each hole—they will fit right in—or place selected items into smaller, individual holders.

Variation

To create a small puppet holder, place dowels that are 4 inches longer than the can into the holes.

☀ Say-Along ☀

This is the way we clean up each day
As we put our scissors away,
I can pick them up by myself
And put them away on the shelf.
Then they'll be ready the very next day
When we all want to play.

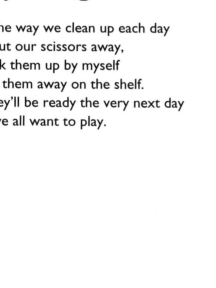

Paper Bag Kickball

Who: Toddlers, preschoolers, and schoolagers

How to Use It

Use the kickball outdoors or in a large indoor area. **Toddlers** will enjoy dropping and throwing the balls into large laundry baskets or boxes. **Preschoolers** and **schoolagers** can make their own balls to practice kicking and throwing skills. In pairs, have older children kick or throw balls back and forth. To encourage cooperative play, devise simple team games using walls or trees as goals. Establish an obstacle course and have the children kick balls around it. You can also use the kickballs with the "Child-Size Game Net" (see page 88) to play a simple version of volleyball.

What It Does

These balls provide easy objects for practicing kicking, throwing, or batting. Playing with them encourages large-motor coordination and hand-eye and foot-eye coordination. Making many balls provides a simple means for encouraging cooperation without competition since each child can have a ball.

Young children love tearing up the newspaper to make these balls (also a hand-eye coordination task). The process teaches how to make an object to use in play.

What You Need

- medium-sized paper bag
- newspapers
- markers and crayons
- stapler
- duct tape

How to Make It

1. Write the child's name in the center of the bag and let each child decorate his own bag for easy identification.
2. Ask the children to tear lots of newspapers into strips or pieces.
3. Stuff the newspaper into the bag until it is about three-fourths full. Mold the bag so it forms a round shape.
4. Fold over the top of the bag and staple it shut. Cover the stapled section with tape to reinforce closure.

Variation

Make smaller balls out of wadded up newspaper formed into a round shape and covered with duct tape.

☀ Say-Along ☀

I can make my very own ball
It isn't very hard at all,
It's really lots of fun to do
'Cuz you get to tear up paper too.

This ball is perfect, do you know why?
'Cuz I can toss it way up high,
It's easy to throw or catch or kick
Or bat around with a kind of stick.

Ball is so much fun to play
I think I'll make one every day.

Paddle Ball

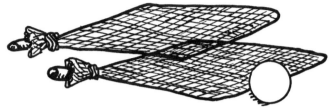

✲ Say-Along ✲

This little paddle sure is dandy
For playing games it comes in handy,
We can use it to hit so many things
Birdies, balloons, or balls hanging on
    strings.

But the neatest games we like to play
Are hockey or golf played our own way,
We can set up our own special playing
    place
And use the paddles to move the balls in
    that space.

It's amazing what these paddles can do,
And if they wear out, we can make
    them new.

Who: Toddlers, preschoolers, and schoolagers

How to Use It

Toddlers and **younger preschoolers** will use these paddles in individual play, pushing light-weight, medium-sized balls around as if putting a golf ball. Place a large box on its side to make a goal to aim at as children gain more control in this activity.

Older preschoolers and **schoolagers** (depending on their experience and abilities) can use the paddle to individually bat a ball up into the air over and over, counting to see how long they can keep it up. Or they may take turns batting and catching a ball with the paddle. For extra fun, suspend a whiffle ball or other ball from a tree branch and use it for batting practice. **Older children** may also form teams and use the paddles to play a form of floor hockey.

Schoolagers might find it challenging to put together a miniature golf course using items such as carpet samples, three-pound coffee cans with both ends removed, and strategically located blocks. Old tennis balls can be used on the course.

What It Does

The paddle balls provide children with large- and small-motor exercise. They build coordination skills and may help in the understanding of numbers. The paddles encourage outdoor physical play and require only free and easily found portable materials. When setting up a miniature golf course, older children learn problem-solving skills and are required to be creative and work as a team. When playing with one another, children also learn turn taking.

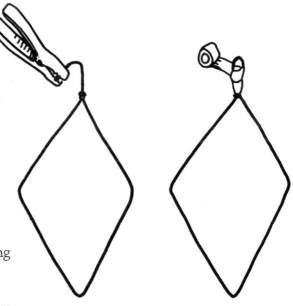

What You Need

For each paddle:

- 1 heavy-duty wire hanger
- pliers
- duct tape
- 1 clean pair of panty hose (for a sturdier and longer-lasting paddle, use two leg-portions per paddle)
- rubber band
- variety of small- to medium-sized balls (such as Nerf, pom-poms, tennis balls, badminton birdie, crumpled newspaper balls, balloons, and whiffle or Ping-Pong balls)
- large cardboard box (optional)

How to Make It

1. Bend the hanger into a round or diamond shape. To create a handle, use pliers to bend down the hook of the hanger and twist it snuggly around its base. Cover the handle with duct tape.

2. Slip the leg portion of the panty hose over the hanger. Wrap a rubber band over the handle to keep the stocking ends tightly in place. Retape with additional duct tape.

3. Store the paddles and balls in a cardboard box.

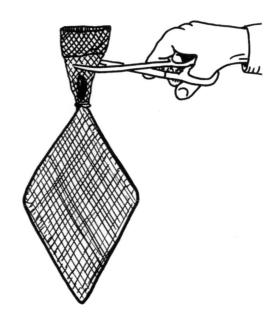

Variation

Create a miniature golf course. Make various obstacles out of old rugs or carpet samples and large coffee cans or plastic buckets with the bottoms cut out. Use large pieces of Mylar or aluminum foil to represent water traps.

Gather old tennis balls and encourage the children to putt through the course.

Following Footsteps Game

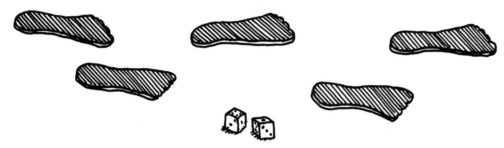

☀ Say-Along ☀

Hi Ho, Hi Ho!
Along the path we go
We'll find our way
This very day
To where, I do not know.

Hi Ho, Hi Ho!
Along the path we go
You toss the dice
Oh boy, it's nice
To hop or skip just so.

Hi Ho, Hi Ho!
Along the path we go
It's so much fun
I think we won
We can play again you know.

Who: Toddlers, preschoolers, and schoolagers

How to Use It

Toddlers will enjoy simply following the footprints placed at an appropriate distance for their stride. For **preschoolers** the feet may be placed close enough together so the children can hop or step from one to another. **Older preschoolers** and **schoolagers**, in pairs, may take turns rolling a die and taking the number of steps indicated on the die. They may also count out loud as they step, or they may want to name and match the foot they land on as right or left.

Place pictures indicating some action to be done (for example, jump rope, do a puzzle, somersault) next to a footprint. The die can be tossed from one child to another after each turn.

Cutout footprints can also show children where to go for new activities. Use them indoors or out. Outdoors allows for longer paths, such as to the back fence or all around the playground.

What It Does

These footprints help toddlers refine their balancing skills. Don't be discouraged if they would rather pick them up and rearrange them on the floor or on the couch. Let them do what is important to them now. The game encourages play with others and taking turns. Hopping, skipping, tossing, and catching all help to develop large-muscle skills as well as an understanding of the concepts of left and right. Using the footprints as paths to activities or the bathroom gives children directions while still allowing for and encouraging independence.

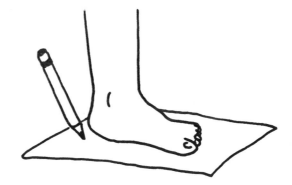

What You Need

- paper for tracing
- pencil
- child's foot or shoe
- vinyl wallpaper samples, thin rug samples, or any material that will lie flat on the floor
- scissors
- die
- good pictures of animal tracks

How to Make It

1. With a pencil, trace a child's right and left foot on a piece of tracing paper.

2. Cut the footprints from the tracing paper. Using the tracings as a pattern, cut the number of feet appropriate for your space and purpose from vinyl samples or other material.

3. Make your own die, following the directions on page 188.

Variations

Make "feet measuring tapes" by taping or paperclipping footprints together (toe to heel). Let the children use the measuring tape to measure things around the room.

If the material you used to make the footprints has a variety of different patterns, mount samples of those patterns on index cards. Have children pick a card and go to a footprint that corresponds to the pattern.

Instead of children's footprints, create animal prints with the children's help (make them larger than life-size). Children can follow the animal prints and pretend to go on a safari in search of the animal.

Workout Weights

☀ Say-Along ☀

Lift those weights up and down
Pick those feet up off the ground,
Marching, marching, all around.
Reach up high, now down low
Wiggle, wiggle, nice and slow,
Marching, marching, to and fro.

Who: Toddlers, preschoolers, and schoolagers

How to Use It

You and the children can do upper body workouts together using weights appropriate to each person's size, ability, and strength. By customizing the weights to each child's ability and strength, all children can participate and succeed. **Toddlers** will enjoy being part of the workout gang with their very light (¼-pound) weights. **Preschoolers** and **schoolagers** can do specific exercises with the weights to work on certain muscle groups. Exercises can be done to the say-along verse or to music or workout videos. **Schoolagers** can participate in making the weights.

Note: Let children choose weights that are comfortable for them. They should use the weights only for as long as they find it to be fun and challenging. Also, before doing any exercise, children and adults alike should do stretching exercises to warm up.

What It Does

Working out helps children learn to enjoy using their bodies, alone or with a group, and encourages a lifelong interest in taking care of themselves. Workouts introduce children to the concepts of personal health and fitness, learning about their bodies (muscles), warming up muscles before exercising, and developing upper body strength.

What You Need

- old and mismatched socks, sleeves from old shirts, or small plastic bottles with secure screw-top covers
- plastic bread bags
- sand or water
- cord or string
- scissors
- duct tape
- scale

How to Make It

Sock or sleeve weight

1. Choose appropriate-sized socks or cut sections of shirt sleeves. If using a sleeve, tie off one open end.
2. Fill the bread bag with clean sand. Use ¼ pound—same as a stick of butter—for toddlers, and up to 3 or 4 pounds for adults. Fill loosely enough so that the children can easily grip the center of the weight.
3. Tie off the bag with string. Slip the bag of sand into the sock or sleeve and securely tie off the open end.

Plastic bottle weight

1. Fill a small bottle with sand or water to the desired weight.
2. Screw on the cover and secure it with duct tape.

Pop Drop

✸ Say-Along ✸

Plop, Plop
Watch the rings drop,
Try to get them over the top.
If they happen to fall on the floor,
Pick them up and try some more,
Just remember to keep track of the
    score.

Who: Toddlers, preschoolers, and schoolagers

How to Use It

This is a great indoor or outdoor game that you can easily adapt to each child's skill level. **Young toddlers** will simply slip rings off and on the bottle. For **toddlers**, demonstrate standing over the bottle and dropping rings over it. As children's skills develop, encourage them to move farther and farther away from the bottle as they attempt to land the rings over the neck of the bottle. Encourage **preschoolers** and **schoolagers** to count the rings that land on the bottle and those that land on the floor.

Older preschoolers and **schoolagers** can use this as a variation of a ring toss or horseshoe game. Place the bottles on the floor and tape circles around them or create a bull's eye on a sheet of plastic. Assign a color to each of these circles that can then be painted onto the plastic.

Schoolagers can form teams, keep track of scores, and make up rules for the game.

What It Does

This game helps develop hand-eye coordination and provides practice in judging distance, position, and direction—all useful perceptual motor skills. The ring toss introduces the idea of taking turns and playing simple games and can provide practice in counting and simple scorekeeping. It can introduce schoolagers to the idea of teams, designing and organizing a court, and deciding on rules.

What You Need

- large plastic soda pop bottle with cap
- funnel and scoop
- sand or water
- Super Glue
- strong tape
- heavy piece of plastic (such as a shower curtain, plastic tablecloth, or tarp)
- yardstick
- permanent marker
- pencil
- string
- hoops (such as plastic bracelets, large drapery rings, rings from rolls of tape, or canning rings)

How to Make It

1. Wash bottle thoroughly and let dry. Using a funnel and scoop, fill the bottle with about 2 inches of sand or water to help stabilize it.

2. Glue the cap on securely and cover with strong tape.

3. For the target circles, lay the plastic sheet on a flat surface and place the bottle in the center. Trace around it with a marker. This is the bull's eye. To draw the other circles, tie one end of a piece of string to a pencil. With one person holding the pencil securely in the bull's eye, a second person can mark every 8 to 10 inches from the center of the circle by tying the marker to the string and drawing perfectly round circles.

Variation

Use smaller bottles to make a bowling game. Draw circles on a piece of plastic to indicate pin locations. Use a rubber or plastic ball. Children can make up their own scoring system by assigning point values to the pins.

Child-Size Game Net

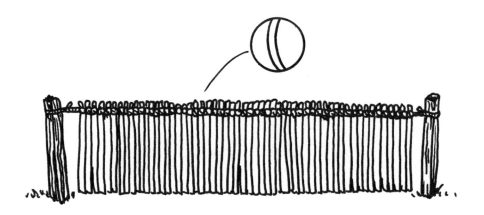

Who: Toddlers, preschoolers, and schoolagers

How to Use It

You can use this net indoors or out and adjust it to children's interest, size, and throwing abilities. Start with the net at or slightly above the children's height.

For indoor use, string the net between two doorknobs, chairs, or railings. For outdoor use, string the net between two trees or posts. Attach hooks to the posts or trees for easy setup. Be sure you have an open playing area on either side of the net that is free of objects children could trip over.

Two or more children can throw or bat balls back and forth over the net. Large, soft balls (such as Nerf balls, beach balls, or balloons) work best. For batting, try badminton birdies, yarn balls, or newspaper balls (see "Paper Bag Kickball," page 79). You can also use this net to cordon off a driveway play area or to set aside an area for temporary play, such as for riding trikes.

☀ Say-Along ☀

Hit, hit, hit the ball
Over the net, watch it fall,
Can you send it back to me?
Over or under, what shall it be?
In playing games, here's what we do:
First send it to me, then it's back to you,
Playing a game is a fun way to learn
What it means to take a turn.

What It Does

This net encourages cooperative play with others. It introduces simplified game-playing concepts, rules, and techniques such as throwing balls over and under the net, rolling under the net, and bouncing and batting balls with hands or a paddle. Adults can introduce some ideas and procedures for play and let children practice and develop them in their own way. Rolling or tossing balls back and forth provides practice in judging distance and speed as well as in taking turns. Simple ball games also promote the development of hand-eye coordination and the development of throwing and catching skills. Using the net to help define space promotes safe use of space.

What You Need

For a 10-foot space:

- 3-yards of wide elastic material for the net frame
- material for the net (such as an old bed sheet or shower curtain)
- scissors
- yardstick

How to Make It

1. Cut or tear 60 streamers (each about 30 inches long x 1 to 1½ inches wide) from a bed sheet or other material.

2. Starting at the center of the elastic, tie the streamers to the elastic so at least 2 feet of streamers hang down and there is about a half inch between each. Leave enough space at each end of the elastic for tying it around trees, posts, or doorknobs.

A Nesting Ball for the Birds

How to Use It

Springtime—when birds migrate and look for good places to build nests and raise their young—is a perfect time to help children become aware of what goes on in nature. **Toddlers** will love watching birds as another interesting new discovery. You can enhance their experience with simple picture books featuring birds, fledglings, and nests.

Preschoolers and **schoolagers** can help make the nesting ball by looking for nest-building materials. When the ball is completed they can look for a place to hang it, such as a tree, where the birds will find the nesting materials and the children can watch as the birds pick at the contents and fly off to build their nests. Talk about how and where the birds build their nests. Explain that we now need to help birds find nesting material since people are often living on the land where birds used to find their materials. Encourage **schoolagers** to find a nesting project to observe and write about.

What It Does

As they see birds fly to and from the nesting ball, children will be introduced to the concept of flight as another means of locomotion (this discovery is often tied to a fascination with airplanes). Older children learn how the birds make their homes and care for their young. These activities provide ways to help children preserve nature, do careful observations, and learn how to record and tune in to the environment around them. Reading and writing about a topic develops language skills and introduces children to bird watching, which can become a lifetime hobby. It also helps develop curiosity about these fascinating creatures.

❈ Say-Along ❈

Springtime is the time of year
When all the birdies reappear,
They look for things to build their nest
And chatter about which spot is the best.

Let's make a ball for the birds to use
With lots of things for them to choose,
Lint and ribbons, strings and such
To give their nest a finishing touch.

See how they hurry to and fro
Pecking at things as they go,
It's fun to watch them as they fly
And we'll check for eggs by-and-by.

What You Need
- nest-building materials
- mesh bag
- string for hanging ball

How to Make It

1. Have children collect suitable nesting materials. Consider using bits of yarn, ribbon, string, dog hair brushings, and lint from a clothes dryer.
2. Stuff the nesting materials into the mesh bag. Bags from onions, potatoes, avocados, garlic, or other vegetables work quite well. Tie the bag closed with string.
3. Hang the ball from a tree branch or other structure that is within easy sight of the children and where the birds can pick at it.

Do-Able

A Home for the Birds (finger play)

Five little birds without a home *(hold up five fingers)*
Five little trees in a row *(raise hands high over head)*
"Come build your nest in our branches tall *(cup hands)*
And we'll rock you to and fro." *(rock the nest)*

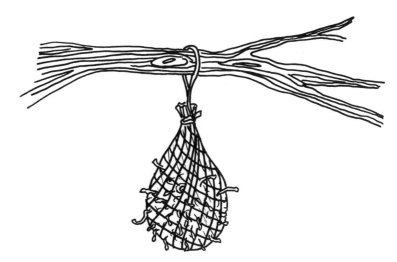

Bottle Bird Feeder

❋ Say-Along ❋

Look at the feeder
What do you see?
Birdies eating
1, 2, 3.

Watch how they peck
At each little speck
Moving their tiny beaks

Then down on the ground
They go hopping around
It looks like the birdfeeder leaks!

Who: Toddlers, preschoolers, and schoolagers

How to Use It

Toddlers will enjoy watching birds at the feeder. **Pre-schoolers** and **schoolagers** can help clean the bottle and, depending on their skills, help prepare the feeder and fill it with birdseed. Talk with the children about the importance of taking care of the creatures. Children can keep track of the different birds that show up at the feeder and note the differences in the way they look and sound and how different birds select different seeds for their diet.

What It Does

This activity promotes children's interest in nature. It gives them an opportunity to actively take responsibility for things in their environment. Children will learn how other creatures eat differently from themselves and one another. While helping to make the feeders, children refine small-motor skills and hand-eye coordination.

What You Need

- plastic pop bottle with cap
- permanent marker
- utility knife
- scissors
- strong cord or string (24 inches minimum)
- birdseed
- dowel (optional)

How to Make It

1. Have children wash and dry the bottle.
2. With the marker, draw an outline of two openings 2 inches up from the bottom on opposite sides of bottle; the opening should be about 2 inches tall and 2 inches wide. With the utility knife, start to cut along each of the lines. Let the children use scissors to complete the openings. Dry the inside of the bottle.
3. If desired, cut two holes the size of the wooden dowel below the feeder opening and insert the dowel through the openings to act as a perch for the birds.
4. Tie the string securely around the neck of the bottle. Fill the bottle with birdseed and hang it where it will be visible, from a window, if possible.

IV.
Preschoolers

Letter Lineup

Who: Preschoolers

How to Use It

Children match the individual letters to the same one on the file folder. They can play individually or as a small group, with each child taking a turn picking a letter to match. Include more than one match for each letter, if you want.

Encourage the children to tell you what they know about each letter (for example, "My name begins with the letter *b*"). Look for other examples of letters around your room (in signs, book titles, cereal boxes) and identify the corresponding letter on the file folder.

What It Does

This game helps children become familiar with letters by playing with them and matching how they look. It encourages children to become more aware of letters in their environment and teaches letter recognition and matching.

The variations (see below) aid initial sound recognition and word-letter associations. All of these visual- and auditory-discrimination tasks help children get ready to read.

What You Need

- construction paper
- scissors
- file folders
- glue stick
- clear contact paper
- plastic bag
- file cards and pictures to make cue cards

❋ Say-Along ❋

So many letters I can see
We can match them quick as can be,
Try to find the letter C
And here is one we call V.

B is for baby, bat, or ball
T is for the trees so tall,
Letters form the sounds of words we say
When we talk together every day.

How to Make It

1. Trace letters of the alphabet on construction paper or use preprinted letters that appear on wrapping paper or in magazines. Cut out the letters. Make sure you have an identical pair of each letter (per set).

2. Glue one letter from each set to the inside of a file folder in random fashion (for young children, use only a few letters). Cover the inside of the folder with clear contact paper.

3. Spread out another piece of contact paper, sticky-side up. Place all remaining letters on the contact paper. Cover with another piece of contact paper to enclose the letters.

4. Cut out the letters from the contact paper, including the internal parts of letters (where it can be done easily) and match with the letters on the file folder. When not in use, place the letters in the plastic bag to store.

Variation

For older children, add a set of cue cards with pictures on them. Have the children match the card to the letter associated with the initial sound of the object pictured (for example, ball matched to the letter *b*). Have children think of words that begin with specific letter sounds.

Wrapping Paper Match-Ups

☀ Say-Along ☀

Here's a puzzle that's really neat
It's full of pictures from Sesame Street,
Do you know who I'd like to meet?
The one who always wants something
   to eat.

Here's another game that's fun to do
We'll match up the friends of Winnie-
   the-Pooh,
These games are really fun to play
But remember to put the pieces away.

Who: Preschoolers

How to Use It
As an independent activity, children match the individual pictures to those on the master playing board.

As a small group activity, distribute pictures to a few children and place the master playing board in the center of the group. Ask questions about the pictures on the board. The child holding the card that answers your questions puts it on the board. Questions can be simple ones asking for a specific object or more difficult ones requiring the child to think about the pictures. For example, for trucks or vehicles, you could ask "Who has a truck that carries loads of dirt?" or "Who has the dump truck?"

What It Does
This game helps children recognize likenesses and differences and learn about ways of classifying things. It helps the development of language and thinking skills as well as the ability to listen and follow directions. Make each game relate to as many topics as possible. Images of all types of animals, toys, vehicles, flowers, rocket ships, desserts, school, or party scenes are available on wrapping paper, wallpaper, and patterned contact paper.

The questioning process can help children learn about the many different ways information can be organized and to help develop skills using some criteria to put information into logical or useful groupings. For example, in a game about animals (as pictured), ask for those with tails, those that have wings, or those that are pets. Discuss with the group how some things can fall into more than one category.

What You Need

- 2 sets of pattern found on wrapping paper, wallpaper, or patterned contact paper
- scissors
- tagboard
- glue
- clear contact paper
- envelope or plastic bag
- paper clip or tape

How to Make It

1. Cut out two complete sets of all pictures. Having eight or nine different pictures works best. Glue one set of pictures to a piece of tagboard. Glue the other set to another piece of tagboard.

2. Cover both boards with the contact paper.

3. For playing pieces, cut out the individual pictures from one of the boards. Leave the other boards whole to use as the master playing board.

4. When not in use, store the pieces in an envelope or plastic bag. Paper clip or tape the envelope to the master playing board.

Look-alikes

☀ Say-Along ☀

1, 2, 3 in a row
That's the way these pictures go;
Study the first box with care
Then try to find the exact same pair.
These pictures can fool you, they're quite tricky
So you have to learn to be very picky;
Be sure each row is exactly the same
'Cuz that's the way we play this game.

Who: Preschoolers

How to Use It

Children complete each row with pictures that match. One or two children can play. Place all the cards face down on the table. Children take turns picking a card and finding its matching object on the master playing board. Play continues until all of the cards are used and the rows are complete.

For **older preschoolers**, use wrapping paper pictures or stickers that are very similar to make the game more difficult.

What It Does

This game encourages children to look for similarities and differences and to pay attention to details. It provides practice in working from left to right and helps develop concentration, memory, and interest in finishing a task—all of which are pre-reading skills. It also offers a simple, noncompetitive game to help teach taking turns.

Children from two and a half to three years old can identify and match pictures on the board. Pattern discrimination games are suitable for four to five year olds.

What You Need
- wrapping paper or stickers
- scissors
- ruler
- marker
- glue
- index cards, 5 x 8 inches
- clear contact paper

How to Make It

1. Cut out three sets of each pattern or design in the wrapping paper or use three sets of stickers.

2. To make the master board, draw lines on the file cards, making squares the size required for the pictures or stickers. Glue a picture or a sticker in the first box of each row. Cover with clear contact paper.

3. To make the game pieces, mount the remaining pictures or stickers onto file cards. Cover with contact paper. Cut out the pictures or stickers in individual squares that will fit the boxes on the master playing board.

Note: Recycle used wrapping paper for this game. Suitable paper contains small pattern prints of similar size, but slightly different in some way (for example, different color, object variation, or pattern). Wrapping paper with five or more different images (as opposed to designs) works best. For example, wrapping paper with small toys in boxes; hearts and flowers in a squared-off design format; and rows of small trucks, animals, clothes, and snowmen.

Suitable stickers would be ones that are similar to one another, such as various types of butterflies or fish, decorated hearts, or flowers.

Variations

Encourage the children to use the cards to play a game like Old Maid. They can pick cards from one another to make pairs.

Have the children lay out the cards, face down, and play Concentration as described in "Picture Partners" (see page 126).

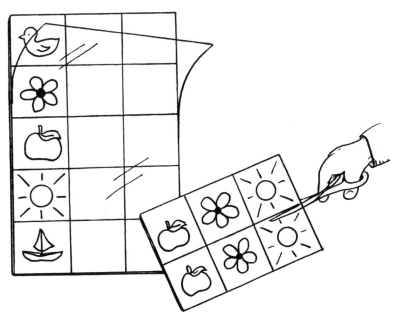

Shape Finders

Who: Preschoolers

How to Use It

The child finds a small card with the shape on it that completes each sequence and places it in the empty box on the larger card. One child can play as an independent activity, or two to four children may play as a type of bingo game.

Instructions for Bingo: Make several larger game cards and matching cards. Give players one or two of the larger game cards. Put all the smaller pieces in a pile. Children take turns picking the small cards and seeing who has the matching picture on their larger card. You may want to serve as a caller or demonstrator the first few times the game is used. Continue playing until all the cards are completed.

What It Does

This game helps children learn to recognize a sequential pattern and provides practice in using clues such as color or shape to help solve a problem. It encourages the development of "thinking" or cognitive skills as a child tries to decide what comes next. The independent activity provides a quiet, challenging game for the child who likes to work alone on intellectual problem-solving tasks. The bingo game provides an opportunity for taking turns and cooperating in those same problem-solving tasks.

☀ Say-Along ☀

To play this game you must find
The shape that would come next in line.
First look at the pictures in each row,
Is there a pattern that you know?
Then look at the little cards to see,
Which one you think it might be.
The shapes and colors are your clues,
To help you decide which one to choose.

What You Need

- unlined index cards, 5 x 8 inches
- stickers or colored coding dots
- marker
- clear contact paper
- Velcro
- scissors
- envelope

How to Make It

1. On four to six of the index cards, arrange the stickers or dots in four rows, using a different sequence in each row.

2. Draw lines between each row and a box at the end of each row for answer pieces. Cover the cards with clear contact paper. Mount a small piece of Velcro in the answer box.

3. To make the answer pieces, draw lines on additional index cards to create small squares that will fit into the answer boxes. Inside box, mount the stickers or dots that correctly complete the sequences and cover with clear contact paper.

4. Cut the answer cards into individual pieces. Mount small pieces of Velcro on the back of the answer cards. Store the pieces in an envelope.

Sort It!

☀ Say-Along ☀

Do you know what these tongs can do?
They can help pick things up for you.
My mother uses tongs for things that
    are hot
When she picks them out of a great
    big pot.

I think that they are fun to use
But be careful or you might lose
The very thing that you are holding
Before you get it to the spot you're
    loading.

Who: Preschoolers

How to Use It

Put out a muffin tin and a container of small plastic beads. Have children sort the beads into the cups by color, matching the bead color to the "cue color" circle in each cup.

Change the sorting activity by varying the sorting criteria. For example, liners set in the muffin tin can be made to indicate to sort by quantity (number 1 through 8 in the bottom of the cups), shapes, outlines, or colors of specific items such as buttons.

You can vary the activity by adding tweezers or small tongs to use to pick up the beads or other items. Tweezers work best for smaller items, tongs for larger ones.

What It Does

This activity offers a way to use common materials like beads and buttons to teach specific concepts, such as matching colors or shapes. Sorting tasks help children learn to recognize identifying characteristics (likenesses and differences) and to then organize these items by various categories. This helps children learn to pay attention to details and sharpens perception skills. Picking up small objects helps develop small-motor coordination.

Using tweezers or tongs provides the challenge of learning to manipulate a tool requiring both hand-eye and small-motor coordination, making the task more interesting than the sorting alone.

What You Need

- six- to eight-cup muffin tin
- construction paper
- scissors
- pencil
- items to sort (such as colored plastic or wooden beads, buttons, counting cubes, beans, pegs, plastic shapes, counting bears, large marbles, lids, or poker chips)
- tweezers or tongs
- bowls

How to Make It

1. Trace the bottom of the muffin tin on colored construction paper that closely matches the colors of the items being sorted. Make one circle from each color.

2. Cut out the circles and place one inside each cup.

3. Fill small bowls with many multicolored beads or other materials to sort.

Pizza Pinups

✹ Say-Along ✹

Look at one section carefully
How many pictures do you see?
Let me count them, 1, 2, 3,
Find the clothespin that says 3
Clip it on where it should be.

Now let's look and count some more
Let's find out where to put this 4,
Now what numbers should we do?
You do 5 and I'll do 2,
We'll take turns until we're through.

Who: Preschoolers

How to Use It

Use this game in an activity area that involves numbers or as a small group or individual activity.

Tell the children to look at one slice (or section) of the pizza board and count how many pictures they see in it. Have a child find the clothespin with the matching number on it. If the child is not sure of the number, turn over the clothespin and count the dots to see if the numbers match. Then clip that clothespin to the corresponding pizza slice. Continue until all the clothespins are attached.

Children will be able to do this activity independently after being shown the procedure.

What It Does

The game helps children learn correct numerical value by giving them practice in counting and matching, and it provides practice with the idea that each number stands for a corresponding quantity. Manipulating clothespins promotes small-motor development. The game also provides an opportunity for a few children to work cooperatively to complete a task and to help one another as needed in identifying the numbers.

What You Need

- cardboard circles (any size)
- small stickers or coding dots
- markers
- ruler
- clip-style clothespins and a container to hold them
- clear contact paper

How to Make It

1. Draw dark lines on the cardboard circles, dividing it into eighths.

2. Draw pictures or arrange stickers in each section of the board for quantities from 1 to 8.

3. Write the numerals 1 to 8 on clothespins. On the opposite side of each clothespin, draw the corresponding number of dots (or use small coding dots).

4. Cover the cardboard circles with clear contact paper. Store the clothespins in a suitable container.

Variation

Create similar games to match colors or shapes. For older preschoolers or schoolagers, make an identification game using pictures of objects that begin with the same letter in each section of the cardboard circle. Write the corresponding letter on the clothespin.

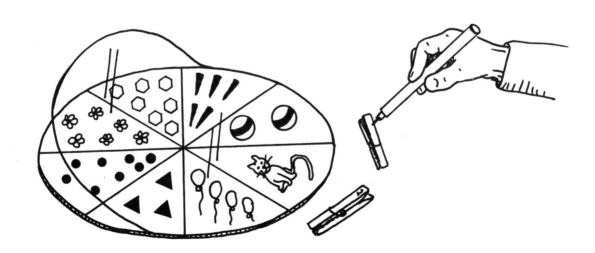

Numbers Galore

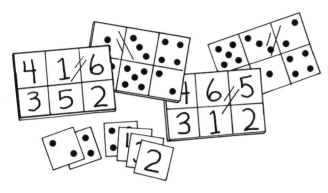

☀ Say-Along ☀

These games are called Numbers Galore
'Cuz we count and count and count
   some more,
Look how many different ways
We play these games on different days.

Sometimes the game is called Bingo
And we cover up the numbers we know,
Another time it's mix and match
The cards and numbers in this batch.

We all remember to take a turn
And look at all the numbers we learn,
Sometimes it's just fun to play
Spread these cards out any old way.

Who: Preschoolers

How to Use It
You and the children can play numerous games with these sets of cards.

Noncompetitive Bingo: Four children each have a bingo board and counters. Call out the number and have the children cover that number with a marker. Since all the boards have the same numbers on them, all of the children will finish at the same time.

Concentration: Place the cards face down and have the children find the pairs. Children can play this game with either the dot cards or the numeral cards.

Match-Ups: Match the dot cards to the bingo boards or the numeral cards to the dot cards.

What It Does
Because this game has many possible adaptations, it encourages adults and children to try out new ideas and illustrates how one item can be used in various ways. The game teaches numeral recognition, as well as matching like-sets and matching numerals to the correct quantity. It encourages counting from 1 to 6 and introduces the concept of number sets (4 cards each with the number 3 on them are a set of 3s). It also encourages playing some games in noncompetitive ways, allowing all players to participate simultaneously. You and the children can also use this game in combination with counters or dice to make other matching or counting games.

What You Need
- 3 pieces of tagboard (12 x 18 inches each)
- ruler
- marker
- black coding dots
- scissors
- clear contact paper
- pencil
- bingo markers (such as pennies, buttons, or poker chips)
- box to hold the cards, numerals, markers

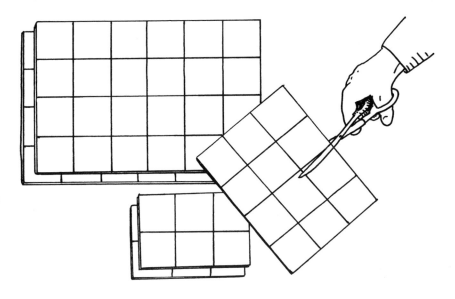

How to Make It

1. Using a ruler, mark off 24 3-inch squares on each of the three pieces of tagboard.

2. On one of the large pieces of tagboard, make four sets of dots that represent numbers 1 through 6. Cover with clear contact paper.

3. On the other piece of tagboard, print four sets of the numerals 1 through 6 in 24 squares. Cover with clear contact paper and cut into 3-inch x 3-inch playing cards.

4. To make the bingo cards, cut one piece of tagboard into 4 9- x 6-inch pieces.

5. Mark off 6 squares on each side of the card. On the first side, place 1 to 6 dots in the squares, varying the placement on the cards but keeping patterns for each number the same as on the large card. On the reverse side of the bingo cards, write the numerals 1 to 6 in the squares. Cover the large pieces of tagboard and the bingo cards with clear contact paper.

Number Game Variations

To Use with Plastic Numerals: Match the plastic numerals to either the dot side or the numeral side of the bingo cards. Plastic numerals can be placed in a row and all the playing cards that match that numeral can be placed in that row also.

To Use with Counters: Add counting items such as buttons, pennies, or poker chips, and place the appropriate number of counters on either side of the bingo cards.

To Use with Playing Cards: Place a label or sticker of the suits (club, heart, diamond, and spade) on each bingo card. Divide a deck of cards and place the cards from aces through sixes face down on the table. Children draw a card from the pile and find its place on the bingo card, matching the suit and number.

Bottle Cap Counters

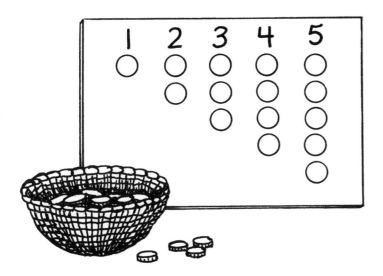

Who: Preschoolers

How to Use It

Use in a variety of counting and matching games. For a number matching game, have the children arrange bottle caps in rows, counting out the appropriate number. Use numbers 1 to 5 for younger children (which will require 15 bottle caps), and add 6 to 10 for **older preschoolers** (which will require 55 bottle caps). Make a color matching game by writing each numeral in a different color. Children then use bottle caps that match the indicated color.

What It Does

This game helps children learn about numbers by actually counting out the correct quantity for each numeral.

The variations (see below) provide practice in learning to recognize and match colors, which encourages visual-perception skills. The variation games also provide activities adapted to differing ability levels. These games are simple, number-color matching and sorting activities for younger children. They can provide an opportunity for children to use their imaginations and create their own games with a colorful and readily available material.

What You Need
- tagboard
- markers
- 15 milk bottle caps
- basket

☀ Say-Along ☀

These bottle caps are a lot of fun
We can count them one by one,
One way to count them that I know
Is to arrange each number in a row.

The higher the number, the longer
   the row
Look and you will see it's so.

For the first numbers we are able
To fit the rows right on our table,
But if you want to do lots more
You'll have to spread them on the floor.

How to Make It

1. Write the numerals 1 to 5 across the top of the tagboard. Under each numeral, use a bottle cap to trace the appropriate number of circles. (For color matching games, use colored markers to write numerals and trace circles.)
2. Store the milk bottle caps in a small basket.

Variations

Sort the bottle caps by colors into matching bowls.

Write the numerals 1 to 5 on pieces of paper. Fold up the pieces and place them in a bowl. Have the children draw a number and arrange that number of bottle caps on the board or on the table next to the number. Add larger numbers (6 to 10 and higher) for older children.

Encourage children to make up their own games. Use poker chips instead of or in addition to bottle caps.

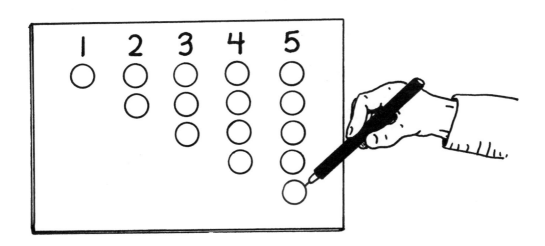

Counting Circles

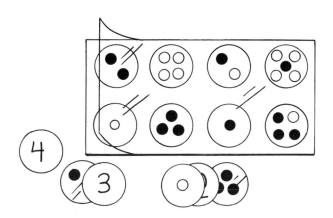

How to Use It

This activity is a number and color matching game that is appropriate for individual or small group use. In a small group game, place the master playing board in the center and deal the playing cards around the group. Point to a circle on the master playing board and describe it by color and number (for example, "green 4s"). All of the children with those cards place them on the matching master playing board space. Play other games using a single category (for example, "all red" or "all 2s"). The children with cards matching the category place them on the board.

Use this activity to match sets. Match the coding dots to corresponding sets of coding dots or to the appropriate numeral written on the other side of the playing cards.

❋ Say-Along ❋

How many dots can this be? (*point to the circle with 3 dots*)
Is it 4 or is it 3?
Let's count together and we'll see
Ready now, 1, 2, 3. (*point to each dot*)

3's the number we're looking at
So find some circles just like that, (*point to the pile of circles*)
Put them in this special place
Then look for numbers for another space.

What It Does

This activity offers practice in comparing and matching sets of dots by number or color. It also helps children associate specific numerals with the corresponding quantity. With direction, this activity helps illustrate number concepts behind words such as *more, less,* and *many.* It also provides a simple game that encourages children to take turns and pay attention while playing with and learning about number concepts.

What You Need
- 2 pieces of tagboard (8 x 16 inches each)
- ½-inch coding dots in a variety of colors
- marker
- scissors
- 3-inch circle pattern
- clear contact paper

How to Make It

Master Playing Board

1. Trace two rows of 3-inch diameter circles on one piece of tagboard.
2. Place coding dots in the circles. Use different colors for each circle, but keep the dot arrangements consistent for each number. Cover the entire playing board with clear contact paper.

Playing Cards

1. On the other piece of tagboard, trace two rows of 3-inch diameter circles. (You may make as many pieces as you wish, because more than one circle can match the circle on the master playing board.)
2. Place coding dots in the circles to match the circles on the playing board (both in colors and number of dots used). Cover cards with clear contact paper and cut out each circle.
3. On the back of each circle, write the numeral that corresponds to the number of dots. (For younger children, write the numeral in the same color as the dots. For older children, write the numerals in black.) Cover the backs with clear contact paper.

Variation

For a larger group or for older children, make additional master playing boards and increase number variations (using numbers 1 to 8). Make additional playing cards as well. Older children could use this as a bingo game.

Visiting the Zoo Board Game

✳ Say-Along ✳

This game is about our trip to the zoo
We saw lions and tigers and
   monkeys too;
When we play this game,
We say each animal's name;
And what is more
We get to roar.

One of the things that was really neat
Was to see how all the animals eat;
Our trip to the zoo was lots of fun
But since that trip is done,
Playing this game is the best we can do
To help us remember our trip to the zoo.

Who: Preschoolers

How to Use It

Two to four players can play this game. You should first play the game with the children to introduce it and promote discussion of the topic.

Place the board and cards in the center of the group. Each player takes turns picking cards and moving a game piece the appropriate number of spaces along the path. If a player lands on an animal picture, the group names and discusses that animal and everyone imitates the sound it makes (for example, a lion's roar). When a card with a snack picture on it is drawn, that player's game piece stays put and the player pretends to eat the pictured snack. The game continues until everyone finishes visiting the zoo and lands on the going home space.

Use this game in preparation for a trip to the zoo or a similar outing (for example, a farm with animals or barnyard animals at the mall). Also use this game for review after the trip.

Very young children may not be interested in the rules of the game but will enjoy moving their game pieces along the path, making the animal sounds, and making up stories about the animals, which may help hold their attention.

What It Does

This game provides an opportunity for children to practice counting as they move their game pieces along the path. It also provides opportunities to discuss the animals, what they do, and the experiences that will be part of the trip. And they get to imitate animal sounds! Not only does this help to better prepare the children for the experience, but it greatly increases language learning by promoting verbal expression and creativity. Playing games also promotes sharing, taking turns, following directions, completing a task, and having fun with others.

What You Need

- large piece of tagboard
- felt-tip markers
- pictures or stickers of zoo animals
- clear contact paper
- 12 index cards, 3 x 5 inches each
- scissors
- glue
- small coding dots
- magazine pictures of snacks
- game pieces

How to Make It

Playing Board

1. Draw a curving path on the tagboard from one corner to the opposite corner. Divide the path into 1-inch squares. At the start, draw an arrow and print the word *Zoo*. At the finish, draw a picture of a bus or car and write *Going Home.*

2. In every sixth or eighth space along the path, place a picture of a different animal.

3. Decorate the playing board with other pictures to look like a zoo. Cover the game board with clear contact paper.

4. For game pieces, use such items as beans, bingo pieces, buttons, flat beads, bottle caps, corks, rocks, spools, thimbles, large washers, and pieces from other games.

Playing Cards

1. Cut each index card in half. On 16 to 18 cards, write a number from 1 to 3. Put the same number of coding dots on each card. Cut out the pictures of snacks and glue to the remaining 6 to 8 blank cards. Consider using magazine pictures of such snacks as ice cream bars, pretzels, apples, and popcorn.
2. Cover the cards with clear contact paper.

Variations

To vary the game, make the playing board from file folders, old place mats, oil cloth, or old game boards covered with contact paper. Make the paths square, circular, diagonal, snail shaped, or any combination of these. Increase the difficulty of the game by using cutoffs or arrows that direct players to longer paths.

To change the tasks, have children match shapes, colors, numbers, rhymes (depicted visually), textures, patterns, letters, or letter sounds to pictures.

To change the format, have the children use dice or a spinner with colors coded to the game board, or have them pull numbers from a sock or box.

Board game themes are unlimited. You can make a game board to introduce or explain any topic from how plants become products in our grocery stores to the route a letter takes from your home to a friend's. Some other examples:

Trips: going to the hospital, fire station, apple orchard, airport, library.

Books: Into Space, The Magic School Bus.

Products: how milk, corn, or potatoes go from a farm to our table, how chairs come from trees, how peanut butter comes from the peanut plant.

Top the Box

Who: Preschoolers

How to Use It

This is an independent activity in which one or two children try to find the number sets that go together.

Spread out the boxes in random fashion so the tops and the bottoms are visible. (The boxes should be different enough in dimensions so that each top fits only one bottom, making the game self-correcting.) After matching the correct bottoms and tops, children may put the indicated number of beads or other items in each box.

What It Does

This game helps children recognize numerals and the quantity each numeral represents. Putting boxes together provides practice using small-motor skills, and recognizing and matching sizes provides practice using perception skills. The game provides an opportunity to discuss and illustrate many concepts such as *shape, fit, open, close, inside, top, bottom, empty, full,* and *how many.*

What You Need

- small boxes with lids of similar size and shape, but different enough so each top fits only one mate (jewelry boxes work well)
- small objects to place inside the box (such as beads, pegs, or buttons)
- markers
- small coding dots or gummed stars
- scissors

How to Make It

1. Inside the bottom of each box, write a numeral from 1 to 6.
2. Write the same numeral on the inside of the box's lid. For older preschoolers, you may omit writing the numerals on the inside of the box's lid.
3. Place the corresponding number of dots or stars on the top of the box's lid.

Variation

Mount matching pieces of colored construction paper inside each box and its lid. Let the children match the colors, or they could use the boxes to sort small objects by color.

☀ Say-Along ☀

Look at all the boxes and try to find
The ones you think are a matching kind,
When you find a bottom and top that fit
Then see how many _____ should go in
   it. (*name the item*)
This little game is fun to do,
And helps us learn our numbers too!

Painter's Palette

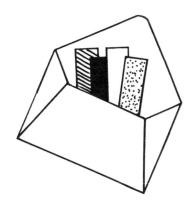

Who: Preschoolers

How to Use It

Have children spread out the color boards and find the pieces that match each color.

For young children, make the boards with very different colors. As skill increases, make and use boards that require more precise color discrimination (for example, use different shades of one color).

For older children, put out large boxes of crayons or colored pencils and paper and see if the children can create shades that match the color boards. Integrate color boards into curriculum for holidays (for example, on Valentine's Day use red and pink) or special days (for example, Purple Day).

Make up games using color samples in various shades of all colors (for example, find the lightest or darkest shade of blue, find the red that matches the crayon).

What It Does

This activity provides practice in matching colors and learning to recognize different shades and tints of the same color. It helps to teach concepts of lighter and darker and encourages visual-perception skills through noticing and paying attention to small differences.

What You Need

- paint color sample cards, 2 of each color
- unlined index cards (5 x 8 inches each)
- glue
- clear contact paper
- scissors
- envelopes
- crayons

❋ Say-Along ❋

Which color do you like best?
I like red better than the rest.
But which red do you mean?
Light red, dark red, or in between?

I'll look at those little cards to see
Which red is the best for me.
Look at all those shades of red!
Maybe I should choose pink instead.

I never knew colors could be so tricky
Red is red, I'm not so picky,
All shades of red look good to me
Like fire engines, valentines, or apples
    might be.

How to Make It

1. Cut apart the paint color samples. Be sure to have two of each.
2. Select colors desired (either different or similar). Glue one set of colors onto an index card. Leave the other set of colors in pieces. Make several sets.
3. Cover the index cards and the individual pieces with clear contact paper.
4. Store the index cards and the individual pieces in envelopes according to their colors, if desired.

Do-Able

Make your own palettes that show the shades of various colors. At the top of a 9- x 12-inch sheet of paper, paint a stripe of one color. Dip the paintbrush in water, wipe the brush against the side of the water dish to remove the excess, and then paint another stripe. The second stripe will be one shade lighter than the first. Keep repeating this process until the sheet is covered with stripes—each one a lighter shade of the same color—until all color is removed. Make similar palettes for many colors and let the children discover which colors are stronger (their color lasts longer) and which ones seem to lose their color faster.

Stop and Go Race Game

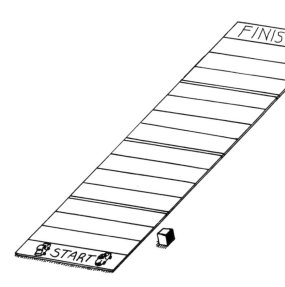

Say-Along

We can have a fun car race
First put your car in the starting place,
Roll the cube and we will see
Red or green what shall it be?

Red means stop—just stay where
  you are
But for each green you can move
  your car,
Along the track toward the finish line
At taking turns we are doing just fine.

The rule that we all need to know
Is red means stop and green means go.

Who: Preschoolers

How to Use It

Two children at a time play this game. Each child chooses a small car to use as a playing piece and places it on the start line. The first player tosses a cube that has red and green sides. If the color is green, that player's car moves ahead one space. If red shows, the player's car does not move. The game ends when both cars have crossed the finish line.

What It Does

This game helps teach children to associate the colors red and green with stop and go. Use it when you are teaching about traffic lights or as part of an interest center about cars, traffic, or transportation. Children love to play with small cars, and this game encourages them to use cars cooperatively in a simple game that models new ways to use cars in play.

Playing simple noncompetitive games gives children practice in taking turns and following the rules—concepts that preschoolers are just beginning to explore and do not fully understand.

What You Need
- 4 sheets of tagboard (8 x 11 inches each) or 4 file folders
- cloth tape
- marker
- ruler
- clear contact paper
- small wooden cube
- paintbrush
- scissors
- red and green paint
- 2 small cars

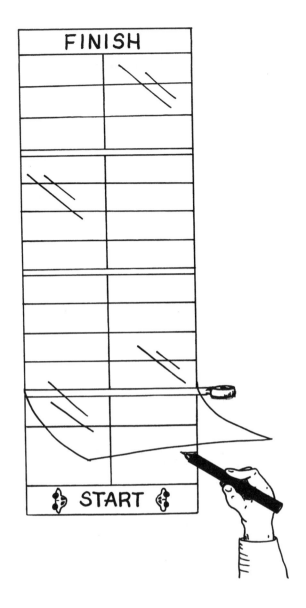

How to Make It

Game board

1. Join the tagboard pieces to one another with cloth tape to form one 8- x 44-inch piece. For strength and durability, be sure to tape both the front and back sides of the seams. Cloth tape allows the board to fold easily for storage.

2. Rule off a section at each end. At one end, print the word *start* and draw two cars. At the other end, print the word *finish*.

3. Draw a dividing line down the middle of the board to form two lanes. Mark off intervals across the board (be sure cars fit into the intervals). Cover the racetrack with the contact paper.

Stop and go cube

Paint two sides of the cube red and four sides green. You can use any small-sized wooden cube, or you can make your own cube from milk cartons (see page 188).

Variation

Make the game board out of oilcloth, heavy vinyl, or an old shower curtain. Use tape to mark off the spaces of the racetrack.

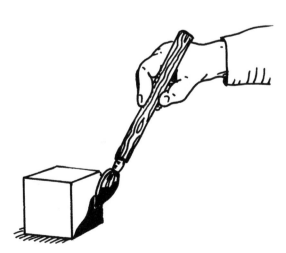

Cracker Game

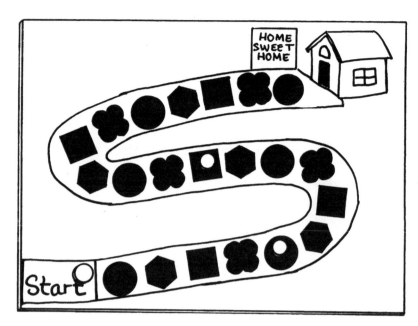

HOME SWEET HOME

Start

☀ Say-Along ☀

This game is such a special treat
'Cuz it also is a game you eat,
Pick a card to move along
Then find the cracker to make you
    strong.
You match different shapes to play
    this game
But when you eat them, they all taste
    the same.

Who: Preschoolers

How to Use It

Use this game board with both small and large groups of children for a variety of games.

For a small group game, place a stack of the playing cards face down. Have children take turns drawing cards and moving their playing piece to the next shape along the path that matches the card drawn. They can return cards to the bottom of the pile after each turn. Each child in turn continues along the path until all players reach "home" place.

What It Does

This game helps develop awareness of shapes in common objects and encourages children to recognize likenesses and differences in shapes. It provides practice at turn taking, playing a simple, noncompetitive game, and following directions.

The variation (see below) promotes social interaction and may stimulate discussion about food-related shapes.

What You Need
- tagboard for game board (12 x 18 inches), cards, and patterns (9 x 12 inches)
- marker
- small objects for playing pieces (such as buttons or beads)
- a variety of different-shaped crackers
- clear contact paper
- scissors or paper cutter
- ruler

How to Make It

1. On the large piece of tagboard, draw the game board, as illustrated.

2. On the other piece of tagboard, trace each cracker shape and cut out the shapes to use as patterns.

3. Use the patterns to trace a sequence of shapes along the path on the game board. Spread them out so you have 20 to 24 outlines on the path. Cover the board with clear contact paper.

4. For the playing cards, measure 2½-inch squares onto the tagboard. Using the patterns, trace each shape in the squares. Make at least four playing cards of each shape. Cover the cards with clear contact paper. Cut out the cards.

Variation

This variation works well as a snack-time game. Arrange the crackers directly on a sanitized board and have the children take turns drawing a card and eating a matching cracker from the game board. Continue until all the crackers are gone.

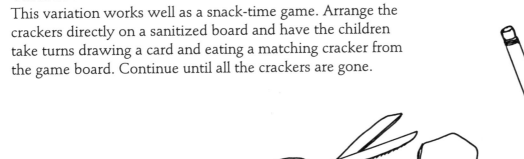

Magnet Mysteries

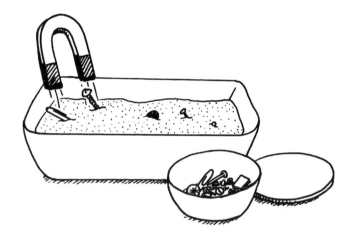

Who: Preschoolers

How to Use It

After an initial demonstration, children bury or hide metal and nonmetal objects in the sand, then use magnets to seek them out. The metal objects must be either iron, steel, or copper for the magnet to work. The magnets should not have to touch the sand but be strong enough to pull out the objects. Strong bar, horseshoe, or "cow" magnets work well. Children can count the items they put into the sand to see if they have retrieved all of them. To catch loose sand, place all of the items used in this activity on a tray or cookie sheet. For storage, simply put the magnets and the objects in the sand bucket and put a lid on it.

This is intended to be an activity that is used by one child at a time. Make extra sets, if desired, for use by additional children. For a group version of this activity, have children bury objects in a sandbox and give several children magnets to see how many items they can retrieve.

What It Does

This activity provides a fun way for children to learn about and experiment with magnets. Hiding the objects provides sensory stimulation. Counting and remembering if all the items are recovered provides children with an opportunity to develop their cognitive and memory skills. Burying objects and removing them from the magnet provides practice in small-motor skills. Experimenting, observing, questioning, and discussing results introduces children to the scientific method of inquiry.

For a variation, include some items the magnet will not pick up. Talk about what happened and why the magnet didn't work on those objects.

❊ Say-Along ❊

We'll bury some treasures in the sand
But we won't dig them out by hand,
There's an easy way to draw them out
While learning what magnets are all
   about.

Just run the magnet above the sand
Anything metal will jump and land
Right on the magnet in your hand,
But if some things still seem to hide
It means they have no metal inside.

It's fun to use this magnet trick
To see what can be picked up quick!

What You Need

- large plastic container with lid
- tray or cookie sheet
- clean sand
- small metal objects (such as nails, screws, paper clips, or ball bearings)
- nonmetal objects (such as plastic and aluminum toys)
- small margarine tub with lid
- strong magnets

How to Make It

1. Clean out the large container and let dry.

2. Fill the container half to two-thirds full with sand and place it on a tray.

3. Collect metal and nonmetal objects and magnets. These items can be placed in clean margarine tubs for storage.

Do-Able

Several good books offer excellent introductions to magnets and many ideas to try with magnets. For starters, look in your library or local bookstore for the following: *What Makes a Magnet,* by Franklin Branley (Harper Collins, 1996); *Playing with Magnets,* by Gary Gibson (Copper Beech Books, 1995); *The Science Book of Magnets,* by Neil Ardley (Gulliver Books, 1991).

Dots to Dinosaurs

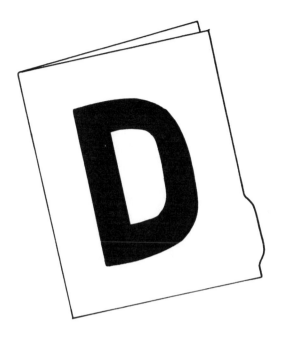

Who: Preschoolers

How to Use It

In this activity, children match a sequence of dinosaur images to a similar sequence of dots. First have children find all the small dinosaurs and put them next to the smallest dot, then have them continue to the medium-sized and largest dots. Be sure to say the words *dots* and *dinosaurs*. Add other small, medium, and large pictures of things that begin with the *d* sound, such as dolls, ducks, dresses, and dogs.

What It Does

This activity teaches auditory discrimination skills by providing practice in matching sounds for the letter *d*. Sequencing by size encourages visual discrimination and problem-solving skills. All of these processes contribute to the children's cognitive development.

What You Need

- file folder
- marker
- small, medium, and large pictures of dinosaurs
- scissors
- glue
- tagboard
- clear contact paper
- manila envelope
- paper clip

☀ Say-Along ☀

Listen to the sound of the letter d
Then find some pictures to give to me;
Dolls and ducks and dogs will do
Dresses, dishes, and dinosaurs, too!

Now find the pictures that are small
This bottom row is for them all; (*point to small dot*)
The big ones go in this top row (*point to it*)
And the rest line up in the middle just so.

How to Make It

1. Write the letter *d* on the front cover of the file folder. Draw three dots along the left edge of the open file folder: one small, one medium, and one large. Leave ample space between dots. Cover with contact paper.

2. Cut out three dinosaur pictures: one small, one medium, and one large. (Wrapping paper, books, catalogs, or stickers are good sources for dinosaur pictures.) Glue the pictures to a piece of tagboard, cover them with clear contact paper, and cut them out.

3. If desired, attach a Velcro strip underneath each dot on the file folder. Mount small pieces of Velcro on the back of each picture. Store the pictures in a manila envelope paperclipped to the file folder.

Variation

Make additional picture cards to match with items beginning with the letter *d* and other letters. For example, for the letter *s,* draw stars (instead of dots) on the file folder, and match to pictures of shells. For the letter *b,* use balls and bears.

Picture Partners

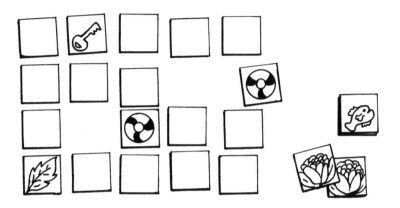

Who: Preschoolers

How to Use It

To use as a game of Concentration for two or three children, place the cards face down on a level surface. Each child takes a turn flipping over two cards so everyone can see the pictures on them. If the pictures match, the child collects the pair and takes another turn. If they don't match, the child turns the cards face down in the same spot and the play moves to the next child. Repeat until the children have paired and collected all cards. (You'll probably need to play initially to introduce the game and the turn-taking process and to encourage the children to remember where cards are.)

A simple game for younger children is to spread out the cards face up and let each child collect one pair for each turn. You can also use the cards as an individual activity in which a child arranges all the cards in pairs.

What It Does

This activity helps children recognize likenesses and differences in pictures. It encourages the development of observation and memory skills, increases concentration, and introduces the concept of a set of items—a pre-math skill. It also encourages taking turns, following directions, and logical thinking.

❋ Say-Along ❋

Would you like to play this game?
Concentration is its name
To play this game you try to find
Two cards that are the exact same kind.

First spread the cards so you can't see
What the pictures underneath might be,
What they are you soon will learn
As everybody takes their turn.

Flip two cards over and if they match
Take them from that great big batch,
If they don't match, back over they go
But what they are we all do know.

The fun part as we keep playing this game
Is to think about which cards might be
   the same,
It can be tricky to remember each card
But if you concentrate it's not so hard.

Make games relating to a particular theme. This helps build vocabularies and illustrates the variety of specific items in the broader category. For example, when playing a game using pictures of trucks, discuss features of cement trucks, dump trucks, moving vans, tow trucks, and pickup trucks.

Note that the matches are harder to find if all the pair sets illustrate the varieties within a single category, such as flowers (a pair of roses, a pair of chrysanthemums, a pair of tulips). Conversely, matches are easier if the pair sets are obviously different (for example, a pair of flowers, a pair of animals, a pair of trucks).

What You Need
- tagboard
- 12 pairs of matching stickers
- scissors
- ruler
- pencil
- clear contact paper

How to Make It

1. Rule off and draw 24 1½-inch squares on the sheets of tagboard.

2. Mount stickers in the center of each square on the tagboard. Be sure to use two of each sticker.

3. Cover the tagboard sheet with clear contact paper and cut out the squares to create 12 pairs of matching cards.

Variation

To make an easier game that produces more matching pairs, make six sets of four matching cards instead of twelve matching pairs. Children still try to find matching pairs, but since there are four matching cards in each set, they get more matches.

V.
Preschoolers
and
Schoolagers

Airplane

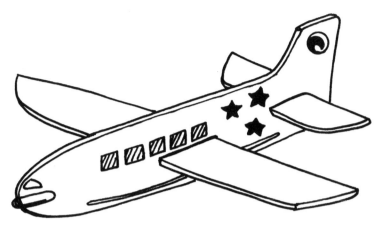

❋ Say-Along ❋

It's fun to make airplanes
And then to fly 'em,
Here are some we made
Would you like to try 'em?

See how we toss them in the air
And they glide and twist around,
Keep watching so you'll know where
They plunge back to the ground.

Who: Preschoolers and schoolagers

How to Use It

Set out Styrofoam trays, an airplane pattern, and a ballpoint pen. Encourage children to press hard as they trace the pattern into the Styrofoam. Vary the size, number, and placement of wings to see how these differences affect flight. Help children make the slits for the wings and insert them to avoid ripping the Styrofoam. **Older preschoolers** and **schoolagers** can make these airplanes and take them outside to fly.

Show pictures of new and old airplanes. Talk about what they look like and how they have changed. Name the parts of the planes. Think about how they fly. Use the verses to add to the discussion.

What It Does

This plane can help illustrate and teach about the principles of flying. You can encourage logical thinking by experimenting with plane construction. By varying the size, shape, and number of the parts and placement of the wings, children get hands-on experience with how these affect flight.

This plane can be an instructive craft activity for studying air transportation. Tracing and cutting encourages small-motor development. Finger plays and discussion about planes encourage language development and memory skills.

What You Need
- tagboard
- Styrofoam trays
- ballpoint pen
- scissors
- paper clips
- clear contact paper (optional)
- markers and stickers (optional)

How to Make It

1. Trace several copies of airplane parts onto tagboard. Cut out the patterns. (Help children as needed.)

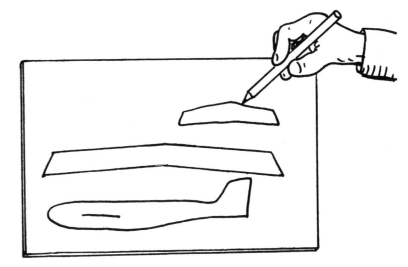

2. Place the patterns on the tray and trace them with a ballpoint pen. Cut out the plane pieces.

3. For longer lasting planes, lay the plane pieces on the sticky side of clear contact paper. Lay another piece of clear contact on top. Press together, making sure the sticky parts of the contact paper are tightly joined all around each piece. Cut out, leaving ⅛ to ¼ inch of contact paper around each piece.

4. Draw two lines in the body of the plane where wings should be inserted. Using the point of a pair of scissors, cut slits along the lines. Carefully insert the wings.

5. Put the paper clip on the nose of the plane. Decorate the plane with stickers, decals, or markers.

Do-Able

Jet-Propelled

Airplanes fly so very high *(look up)*
Jet propelled into the sky, *(move arms up quickly)*
Roar like the wind above tree and cloud *(make noise)*
I wish their engines weren't so loud. *(place hands over ears)*

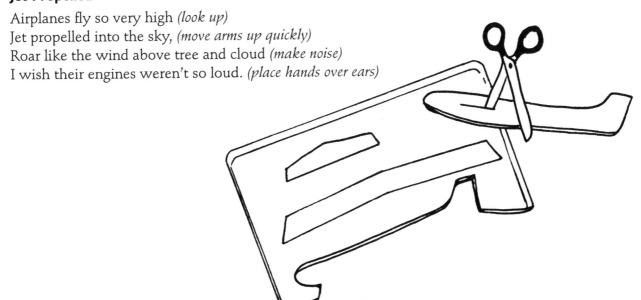

Dot-to-Dot

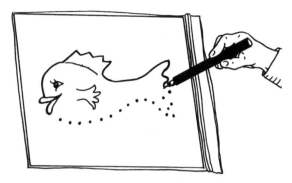

☀ Say-Along ☀

Draw the lines from dot to dot
Then take a look at what you've got,
Can you guess what the picture will be
Finish it up and you will see,
Wipe it off when you are through
And pass it to someone else to do.

Who: Preschoolers and schoolagers

How to Use It

Select a variety of tracing or dot-to-dot pictures and show the children how to insert one picture into a resealable plastic bag. Children trace the picture or complete the dot-to-dot using washable markers or erasable crayons. When completed, the child can use a damp sponge or washcloth to wipe off the plastic bag and do it over again or turn it over and do the other side. Ask the children if they can guess the picture in the dot-to-dot as they work.

What It Does

This activity provides a method to prolong the life of dot-to-dot or tracing pages from coloring books so that children can use them more than once.

Tracing encourages development of small-motor skills and hand-eye coordination. Working with numbered dot-to-dots helps children learn about number sequence. It also helps them learn about following directions and using clues to find an answer. Tracing letters and printing names helps children get ready for writing and builds self-esteem.

What You Need
- numbered dot-to-dot or tracing pages from coloring books
- resealable plastic bags
- tagboard
- wipe-off or washable markers or erasable crayons
- scissors
- glue
- sponges or washcloths

How to Make It

1. Cut out several dot-to-dot or tracing pages from coloring books. (Use pictures of varying difficulty to match the children's abilities.) If the pictures are only on one side of the page, glue the page to each side of a sheet of tagboard.

2. Arrange bags, pictures, markers, and sponges on a table for the children to select and use.

Variation

Make pattern cards of children's names. Insert these cards into bags and let the children practice tracing their names.

Copycat Covers

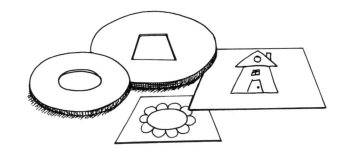

Who: Preschoolers and schoolagers

How to Use It

Children use patterns to trace shapes on paper. They can use the patterns singly or in combination to create designs. Children can color or decorate the shapes or designs in any way they wish. They can use the patterns for spatter, roller, or sponge painting. Ask children what the shapes resemble and what could be added to them to make them look like that object (for example, squares can be houses or blocks, circles can be faces or balls). Use topical patterns, such as pumpkins, hearts, and holiday symbols, for special projects.

School-age children can make their own patterns using scissors and lightweight plastic lids or Styrofoam trays, which are easier to cut.

What It Does

Tracing encourages the development of hand-eye coordination and small-motor skills. This activity helps children learn shapes or pattern discrimination and provides a starting point for child-created pictures that use shapes or symbols in their design. These patterns allow children who want to create a precise shape without adult assistance feel successful.

What You Need

- plastic lids
- pencils
- scissors or X-Acto knife (if made by adult)
- cutting board or cardboard
- markers or crayons
- paper

How to Make It

1. Draw shapes (circle, square, triangle, heart, candy cane) on plastic lids. Consider using lids from ice cream containers or coffee cans. Styrofoam trays are also a possibility.

2. Place the lid on a cutting surface. Use an X-Acto knife or scissors to cut out the shapes.

3. Give children paper, markers, and crayons and the lids to use to make pictures.

☀ Say-Along ☀

See the pictures I can trace?
A pumpkin with a smiley face,
Hearts and flowers all over the place,
And candy canes to color and lace.

It's lots of fun to draw designs
By tracing shapes and connecting lines,
This one looks like a geodesic dome
I think I'll make that my home.

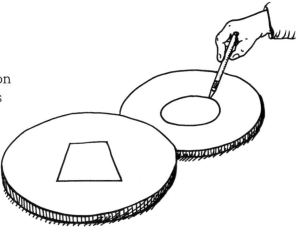

Money Matters

Who: Preschoolers and schoolagers

How to Use It

Children can use this activity to count and match amounts of play money or paper circles ("pennies") that each coin represents (for example, 5 circles equal 1 nickel). Children can make rubbings of coins and then turn them into play money.

Use the cards to see if children recognize the value of specific coins. Hold up the cards with the numeral covered (fold the lower card over the upper one) and see if the children can recognize the coin and tell how many cents (or pennies) it is worth. Use extra sets of the money cards to demonstrate the combinations that make up the value of the larger coins.

What It Does

This activity teaches about the amounts or value represented in each of the coins. Counting out the number of pennies each coin is worth helps illustrate which coins are worth more. It also teaches recognition of coins and the words used for them.

This activity also provides an opportunity to use play money in a unit about banks or in studying about stores. This activity is recommended for children over the age of four.

What You Need

- tagboard: 4 pieces 6½ x 7 inches each; 4 pieces 4½ x 5 inches each
- 42 pennies, 1 quarter, 1 dime, 1 nickel
- glue
- marker
- scissors
- clear contact paper
- paper
- crayon
- small box or sturdy envelope
- tape

How to Make It

1. Glue a nickel to the top of one of the larger pieces of tagboard. Print the word *nickel* under it and the number 5 at the bottom. Glue a dime, penny, and a quarter to the top

Say-Along

One-a-penny, two-a-penny, three-a-penny, four,
Four-a-penny, five-a-penny, that's a nickel more.

Six-a-penny, seven-a-penny, eight-a-penny, more,
Nine-a-penny, ten-a-penny, that's a dime for the store.

of the other three pieces of tagboard. Include the corresponding word and number under the coin. Cover the pieces of tagboard with clear contact paper.

2. On the smaller boards, represent the value of the larger coin by gluing on the equivalent number of pennies (1 for the penny, 5 for the nickel, 10 for the dime, and 25 for the quarter). Cover the boards with clear contact paper.

3. Tape the small card with the pennies to the large card. When you fold up the lower card, the pennies will not show and should cover the number.

4. Use coin rubbings to create play money. Place pennies under sheets of paper and rub over the coins with the side of a crayon. Cut out the rubbings. Store in small box or sturdy envelope.

Variation

Show the different combinations of coins that equal the value of a single coin. Make five cards with five pennies on them and a few with nickels and dimes. For example, the dime card could show 2 nickels or 1 nickel and 5 pennies. The quarter card could show 5 nickels or 2 dimes and 1 nickel.

Do-Able

Four Bright Coins
(Tape coins to large Popsicle sticks and have the children hold up the appropriate coin for each part of the verse.)

Four bright coins shining at me,
The first one said, "I'm a penny, you see."
The second one said, "How do you do?
I'm called a nickel and I'm bigger than you!"
The third one said, "You're both small stuff,
If you want to buy something, you're not enough.
But look at me, I'm small and I shine,
I can buy something 'cuz I'm a dime."
The last coin looked at them all and laughed,
"All of you together don't measure up to me,
'Cuz I'm a quarter, can't you see!"

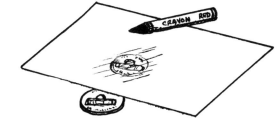

(From *Open the Door Let's Explore More!* by Rhoda Redleaf. Redleaf Press, 1997.)

Tic-Tac-Toe

✸ Say-Along ✸

This is a fun game to know
The name of it is Tic-Tac-Toe,
Pick a card, an X or O
And find a place for it to go.

We'll cover the card as quick as can be
And count how many rows of three,
Xs and Os we'll write down like that
And if there are none, the game goes to
   the cat.

Who: Preschoolers and schoolagers

How to Use It
Two to four children, ages four and up, can play this game. If four children are playing, have an X team and an O team. Divide the X and O cards into separate piles. Children take turns placing Xs or Os on the board, trying to get three of a kind in as many rows as they can. On a score pad, keep track of how many rows there are of 3 Xs and 3 Os. Count rows in all directions—vertical, horizontal, and diagonal. If there are no rows of 3 Xs or Os, give a point to an animal (for example, a cat) drawn at the top of a third column.

    Preschoolers will not try to prevent one another from making complete rows. **Schoolagers** will develop strategies and be more concerned about winning.

What It Does
This activity helps to develop many pre-math and logical thinking skills, including sequencing, sorting same and different, and counting. It also illustrates the concept of a set, because three of the same item (X or O) in a specific order are required to score. Older children may use the activity to develop planning strategies.

The format of this activity makes it possible for more children to play. It also makes it easier to keep track of completed rows and introduces a record-keeping system.

What You Need
- several pieces of tagboard (each 9-inches square)
- ruler
- markers
- scissors
- clear contact paper
- score pad and pencil

How to Make It
1. On the tagboard, draw nine 1-inch squares. Make two boards for team play.
2. Divide two more pieces of tagboard into nine 1-inch squares. On one piece, draw Xs in each square. Draw Os on the other piece. Cover the tagboard with clear contact paper.
3. Cut the Xs and Os into eighteen individual playing cards. Make the playing cards slightly smaller than the sections of the master playing boards to avoid crowding.

Variations
For a portable tic-tac-toe game, mount the master board inside a stationery box. Store the playing cards in the box.

For a magnetic tic-tac-toe game, cut four strips of magnetic tape (each approximately 9 inches in length). Use the strips to form a playing board on a refrigerator door (if metal) or any other iron-based metal surface. Attach small pieces of magnetic tape to the back of each X and O playing card.

Cube-It

Who: Preschoolers and schoolagers

How to Use It

Two children can play this game, or it can be used by one child as an independent activity. The child spreads out all the task cards and reads the numerals or counts the dots to determine the number and color of blocks needed to complete the task. For example, if number 4 has a red square, the child finds 4 red cubes and stacks them on that square. Use numbers 1 through 5 with younger children, saving the larger number sets for those who have mastered the first ones.

What It Does

This activity provides practice in counting objects from 1 to 10 and matching the correct amount to each numeral, which teaches one-to-one correspondence (a crucial step in understanding what numbers mean). It also helps teach organizing by category, such as color, and emphasizes focusing on and completing a specific task. The activity uses simple "reading" and provides a new use for blocks, as well as practice in working from left to right, an important pre-reading and pre-writing skill. The variation (see below) introduces the idea of completing a task quickly.

❊ Say-Along ❊

In this game we count a lot
See how many cubes you've got:
3 in one box and then 1 more
Altogether that makes 4,
5 in the next box in this line
Guess how many that makes? 9!

Fill another card and see
How many cubes that will be,
Here's a card that holds 7
And another that has 11.
Now dump them all and start again
I'm looking for a card with 10!

What You Need

- tagboard sheets (8 x 10 inches each)
- black coding dots (optional)
- marker
- scissors
- clear contact paper
- construction paper
- ruler
- small stackable objects (such as color cubes, flat-surface beads, Lego building blocks, or small colored tagboard pieces)

How to Make It

1. On one sheet of tagboard, rule off three or four rectangle work spaces and print a numeral in the left-hand side of the box.

2. Mount the corresponding number of dots next to each numeral. (You can use the number "0"; just leave the space empty). Make separate sets for numbers 1 through 5 and 6 through 10.

3. Cut 1-inch squares of construction paper in colors that match the color cubes you have. (For numbers from 6 through 10, provide two squares in each box.) Glue on the right-hand side of each box.

4. Cover the counting boards with clear contact paper.

Variation

For older children who like a special challenge, add a minute timer to see how quickly they can complete a card. Encourage the children to count their cubes as they stack them so they use the right quantity for each number.

Dominoes

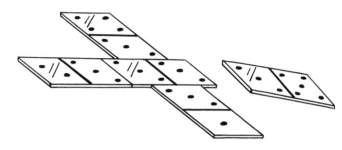

This game we're playing is dominoes
We match the cards into long rows,
We've started in the middle with a
    double 3
So that's what the next one will have
    to be.

Look at your domino cards and see
If you have one to put down with a 3,
After that we add cards at each end
And stretch out the row or make it
    bend.

We'll keep on going till the cards are
    through
Then measure the rows if you want to.

Who: Preschoolers and schoolagers

How to Use It

Two or more children can play this game (play with them at first to introduce the procedures). Have each child draw four to six dominoes from the basket. To begin, place one domino in the center, then take turns adding dominoes that match the number on the free side of the domino. If a player does not have a match, draw from the basket until a match comes up. If all the dominoes are used up and a player does not have a match, the next person who has a match continues. Continue playing until the dominoes are used up or no one can find a match. Count how many dominoes are in each row, if you wish. One child can also play this game as a matching activity.

What It Does

Games with dominoes encourage paying attention to detail, noticing likenesses and differences, and counting—all of which develop matching skills. These games introduce the concept of spatial relations and measurement as the children create extended formations of dominoes. All of these are math readiness skills and contribute to helping children become comfortable using numbers and sets. Playing the game encourages following a set procedure, taking turns, sharing, planning, and having fun with others.

What You Need
- 2 pieces of tagboard (8 x 11 inches each)
- small coding dots (black or other color)
- ruler
- marker
- scissors
- clear contact paper
- basket or box

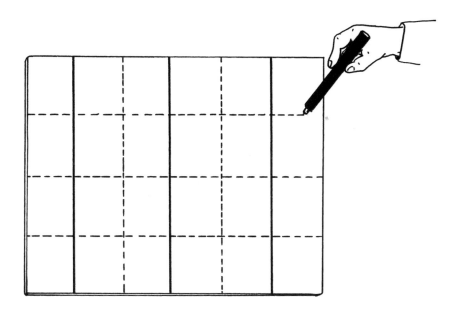

How to Make It

1. On each piece of tagboard, measure and mark off 12 rectangles, approximately 2 x 3⅔ inches each, using dotted lines.

2. Draw a solid line through the middle of each rectangle, running from top to bottom (this line separates the domino into its two parts).

3. Place patterns of 1 to 6 coding dots on each side of the solid lines in each rectangle. Keep the patterns of dots consistent for each number.

4. Cover both sides of the tagboard with contact paper. Follow the dotted lines to cut out each domino.

Variation

Instead of coding dots, use stickers, shapes, or patterns to create picture dominoes. Play in the same manner as described above.

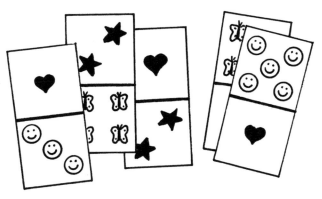

Wipe-Off Scramblers

☀ Say-Along ☀

A _____ is this flower's name (*add flower
name*)
Find another one that's just the same,
Draw a line to connect the two
See how many more you can do.
Then when the whole card is through
Sponge it off and it's good as new.
I think wipe-off cards are really fun
'Cuz I like wiping them when I'm done.

Who: Preschoolers and schoolagers

How to Use It
Place the cards, washable markers, and damp sponges on a
table. Have children draw lines to connect pictures that look
alike. Note children's ability to recognize likenesses and differences and use harder or easier cards. Call attention to
details and identify characteristics in pictures to help children
develop matching skills. When finished with one card, children take the sponge and wipe off the card.

 Make several cards at different levels of difficulty. Children can use these cards individually or as a small group
activity. Make cards in various topics by using different
stickers or pictures.

What It Does
This activity encourages children to practice careful observation to notice likenesses and differences, which is a pre-
reading skill. By choosing some items to match that have
slight differences, children must learn to pay attention to
details. Drawing the lines uses small-motor skills and also
helps reinforce understanding about making comparisons
and connections. The cards provide an activity that can be
made to go with any theme. You can also make cards to
match letters, numbers, colors, or shapes or to teach other
concepts, such as opposites or associations.

What You Need
- pairs of stickers or small pictures from books or
  workbooks (about 10 per card)
- tagboard or index cards (5½ x 8 inches)
- markers or crayons
- small sponges in a bowl
- box or tray to hold materials
- clear contact paper

How to Make It

1. Mount stickers in 2 parallel columns along the side of each piece of tagboard or index card. Leave about 2½ inches to 3 inches of space between rows. (For very young children, place matching stickers within one to two spaces of each other.)

2. Make several different cards. Vary the difficulty by making some cards with slight differences and others with more obvious differences. Cover all cards with clear contact paper.

3. Place the sets of cards and the markers, bowl, and sponges in the box or tray for easy use. You can also use resealable plastic bags for wipe-off cards.

Variations

Following are some additional topics for wipe-off cards:

Things That Go Together: hammer/nail, screwdriver/screw, saw/wood, key/lock, paint/paintbrush.

Things We Use: toothbrush/toothpaste, fork/knife, brush/comb, cup/saucer, sand pail/shovel.

Who Would Eat It: child/toast, dog/bone, cow/grass, Winnie-the-Pooh/honey, bird/worm.

Who Lives There: spider/web, bee/hive, people/house, bird/nest, fish/goldfish bowl.

Opposites: up/down (teeter-totter), hot/cold (fire/ice), big/little (elephant/ant), fast/slow (airplane/turtle), sweet/sour (Popsicle/lemon), soft/hard (pillow/rock).

Sports: tennis racket/ball, baseball bat/baseball, bowling pin/bowling ball, golf club/golf ball, hockey stick/hockey puck.

Cue Me In

Who: Preschoolers and schoolagers

How to Use It

Put cue cards inside each child's deco-rated bag. Vary the number of cards (anywhere from one to ten) according to the age and abilities of the children. Have children walk around the room or yard and collect items that match the cue cards. Samples of cue cards and their use:

- colored strips of paper—children find matching colors
- "shape" cards—children find items of matching shapes
- cards with numerals (for example, number 4 and the same number of dots)—children collect four items

Vary the cue cards in each child's bag so they each are look-ing for a different color or type of item. As the children get used to this game, or for older children, have the cue cards combine tasks. For example, look for colors, shapes, and numbers such as three square blocks or two red beads.

What It Does

Use this activity to teach color, shape, and number recogni-tion. It teaches children to look for and match items, to think about categories, and to make judgments in solving problems (for example, finding things). The activity also helps to stimu-late discussion of all of the above as you talk about and com-pare what children found and collected. Reading the signs on the cue card and following directions encourages children to notice specific characteristics or details of items in the envi-ronment and provides practice in a pre-reading skill.

☀ Say-Along ☀

Look all around and try to find
Items of a special kind,
The notes in your bag will be your clue
Of what it is you have to do.

Collect all the items and when you're
  done
Tell us about them one by one,
A scavenger hunt is another name
For this special kind of game.

What You Need

- paper bags
- unlined index cards
- scissors
- markers
- small coding dots
- construction paper of various colors

How to Make It

1. Have children decorate their bags and put their names on them.
2. Cut small strips of construction paper for color cues. Cut a variety of shapes to use as combined shape and color cues for older children.
3. Make other cue cards by tracing or drawing a variety of shapes or objects on the index cards. Make several of each kind and place them in the bags.
4. To make number cue cards, write large numerals on the cards. For younger children, mount a matching number of dots next to the numeral.

Variation

Consider making specialized cue cards for items in your outdoor environment, such as leaves, rocks, shells, flowers, and grass.

File Folder Fun

Say-Along

To play this game, here's the scoop:
Find pictures that belong to the same
    group,
A group of things that are alike in
    some way
Like clothes to wear or things to play.

Then look at the folders and see if you
    know
Where you think each picture should go,
Talk to each other to see what you think
And you'll get them sorted quick as
    a wink.

Who: Preschoolers and schoolagers

How to Use It

Children file or sort the picture cards into folders according to categories, such as clothes, toys, food, furniture, or things that fly. This game has unlimited possibilities since you can make up endless categories for the file folders, such as letter sounds, colors, shapes, and seasons. You can adapt the game to almost any theme and make it easier or harder depending on the type or complexity of categories chosen.

As the children file the pictures, encourage them to describe and tell stories about them. Count how many objects are in each file. Talk about what other objects they can think of that belong in these categories. Use the files on a table or the floor, hang them from a display rack (see page 184), or use them as part of an office or other dramatic play area.

What It Does

Learning to recognize how different things are grouped together and to make associations about similarities and differences in words and concepts help build vocabulary and word usage skills. Sorting out and discussing the pictures encourage logical thinking and creative expression. All of these are important in the process of learning to read and write.

In doing this activity, the children learn that the pictures represent objects that have meaning and they are "reading" these pictures (or symbols) as they think about sorting them. Using this filing activity in dramatic play incorporates the job of sharpening cognitive skills into play, which is the best way for children to learn.

What You Need
- pocket file folders
- stapler
- scissors
- cloth tape
- sources for pictures (such as old magazines or catalogs)
- unlined index cards (4 x 6 inches)
- glue stick
- marker
- clear contact paper
- large manila envelopes or box to store folders and file cards

How to Make It

1. Cut the file folder in half and staple the pocket along both sides. Cover the stapled sides with cloth tape.

2. Cut out six or more pictures of items in each of several categories (for example, food, clothing, vehicles, animals, or toys).

3. Glue the pictures onto the index cards. Mount one picture from each category on each folder pocket and reinforce it by covering it with contact paper. Print the name of the category above the pocket near the top of the folder. (Older children will enjoy cutting out the pictures themselves and, with direction, can also glue them to the index cards.)

4. Cover the remaining file cards with contact paper and store with the folders in the manila envelope or box.

Variations

Sorting items by categories can be extended to include more complex associations or concepts:

Concept	Picture on Folder
Where would you find it?	things on land, in the sea, in the air
Who would wear it or use it?	adult, child, baby
Where does it go?	kitchen, bathroom, living room, garage
What makes it go or move?	people, electricity, wind, fuel/gas

You can also sort pictures on bulletin boards by various topics, letting the children arrange the items. For example, a bulletin board could feature pictures of a store. Shelves or sections of the store could be labeled specific categories. Older children can use large pushpins to put pictures of items into the appropriate shelves or sections on the bulletin board.

You can also use lids of boxes or candy boxes as sorting trays, labeling them with pictures from each category. Children then sort the pictures into the appropriate groups.

Lids Unlimited

Who: Preschoolers and schoolagers

How to Use It

You can use the lids for many different matching games. Begin by using the lids to talk about how they are alike and different. Select two lids that are exactly alike. Add a third lid that is different from the others in some way and talk about how it is different. For example, begin with two small blue lids, then add a large blue lid. Discuss differences in size, or add a yellow lid and discuss differences in color. Have the children group the lids by a designated characteristic. Make cue cards to use with the lids. Have children select a card and match the lids to the correct circles.

What It Does

This activity provides a lot of learning opportunities for recognizing likenesses and differences; matching color, size, and shape; and categorizing. When used with cue cards, it provides a logical thinking activity that also encourages pre-reading and pre-math skills.

The variations (see below) encourage creativity by using lids in designs or pictures. Younger children may enjoy just manipulating the lids, stacking them together, making towers or rows, or using them to fill and dump.

What You Need

- assorted clean lids or bottle tops
- construction paper
- pencil
- scissors
- index cards (5 x 8 inches)
- glue
- clear contact paper
- marker
- box or basket

☀ Say-Along ☀

Do you know what these lids can do?
They can make designs and puzzles too,
They can fit together in lots of ways
Or make a kind of 3-D maze.

With a bunch of lids and some
  imagination
They can become a neat creation,
Now we never throw them away
Since we found they are so great for play.

*(Be sure to talk about the meaning of the
  words 3-D and maze.)*

How to Make It

1. Clean the lids and tops and allow them to dry. Consider using lids from spice jars, pump hair spray, liquid soap, and milk bottles.

2. Trace the lids onto construction paper of a matching color. Cut out many of each size and color.

3. To make cue cards, glue the circles onto the index cards in a variety of combinations. Also make some that give more specific directions to be followed. Cover the cue cards with clear contact paper.

4. Store cue cards and lids in a basket or box.

Variations

Sequencing Game: Arrange circles in sequences of size and color. Make many different sequences. Have children match the lids to the sequences on the card. Let the children make up their own sequence patterns.

Puzzle or Picture Completion: Make cue cards that contain outlines of various things (animals, birds, or insects work well, as do pictures of snowmen or gingerbread men). Leave spaces for a lid or several lids to complete the picture. Encourage children to notice and talk about what size will complete the picture. Give the children some blank paper and let them draw their own pictures to complete.

Design Cards: Use the circle cutouts of all different colors and sizes to make various free-form design cards. Have children cover the circles with lids to create three-dimensional designs.

Following Directions Game: Use cue cards that give instructions to follow, such as "Stack 4 lids" or "Put 2 blue pen tops in a yellow lid." Children follow directions on each card. Keep directions for younger children very simple. For older children, the directions can be harder (for example, "Put 3 items in 1 top, 4 in another").

Nailboard Design

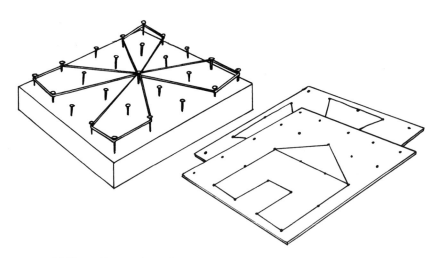

Who: Preschoolers and schoolagers

How to Use It

Children form different designs by stretching rubber bands from nail to nail. Children can make up their own rubber band designs or they can try to follow patterns suggested by cue cards. You can also use these cue cards to prompt particular number tasks ("Make all the rubber bands go around 4 nails" or "How many sets of 5 nails can you enclose with the rubber bands?").

Encourage children to experiment with different shapes as they stretch their rubber bands in different formations (for example, trapezoid, parallelogram, pentagon) and talk about them.

School-age children will enjoy making their own nailboards.

What It Does

This activity stimulates creativity and imagination, teaches hand-eye coordination, and provides practice in using small-motor skills. When used with pattern cards, it can also help teach the children to follow directions and counting. The activity provides practice manipulating sizes and shapes. It also provides practice observing the sizes and characteristics of different shapes and sets of numbers.

Making the nailboards provides a fun project for schoolagers while teaching them about wood-working skills, such as measuring, sanding, and pounding nails. It encourages them to follow a step-by-step process leading to a useful completed product.

☀ Say-Along ☀

Stretch the rubber band so wide
How many nails are inside?
In this design it looks like four
But we can make it a whole lot more.

How many sets of five can there be?
Count them out and let us see,
If we go in each direction
There will be twelve or more for our
    selection.

The designs can go on endlessly
If we use these bands creatively.

What You Need

- piece of wood (8 x 8 inches and 1 inch thick)
- sandpaper
- pencil
- ruler
- 25 2-inch nails
- hammer
- rubber bands in an assortment of colors and sizes
- index cards (3 x 5 inches)

How to Make It

1. Sand the wood to make sure it has no splinters or rough edges.

2. Measure and mark 25 dots on the board about 1¼ inches apart, starting 1 inch from the outer edges of the board (there should be five nails in each row). Hammer a nail about halfway into the board at each dot.

3. To make design cards to use with the nailboards, use markers that are the same color as the rubber bands to draw patterns on the index cards. Make shapes or simple objects made up of straight lines, such as a house, flag, or a zigzag-type pattern.

Variation

Make larger boards using more nails. Boards with 100 nails (10 rows of 10 nails each) are useful for teaching number concepts.

Banjo

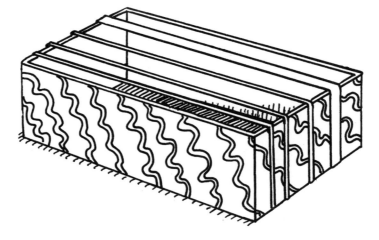

☀ Say-Along ☀

I can play my old banjo
And sing along with E, I, O;
Strumming on my old banjo.
Play it high, play it low
Play it fast, play it slow
Strumming on my old banjo.

I can play my old banjo
And sing along with E, I, O,
Plucking on my old banjo.
Play it high, play it low
Play it fast, play it slow
Plucking on my old banjo.

Who: Preschoolers and schoolagers

How to Use It

Add this banjo to a rhythm band collection and let children strum during a music activity or use it independently to accompany recorded music. Children can also use this instrument as a prop in dramatic play. **Older preschoolers** or **schoolagers** can use this instrument in talent show presentations. For added interest, set up a recording studio play area.

Use this instrument to experiment with sound. Vary the size of the boxes and the thickness of the rubber bands. Notice the effects of different combinations of rubber bands and different ways of playing them.

What It Does

This instrument enhances enjoyment and appreciation of music and provides children with a means of actively participating in musical activity. It focuses attention on some of the basic elements of music, such as tempo, rhythm, pitch, and quality of sound. It also offers a way of experimenting with what factors help produce sound (vibration, tautness of string, thickness of string, size of open cavity). Children learn that the way an instrument is played can change the sound (strumming versus plucking). Use of this instrument can help teach words such as *high, low, slow, resonance, vibration, pluck,* and *strum.*

What You Need

- sturdy rectangular-shaped boxes or plastic containers (various sizes)
- rubber bands of different thicknesses
- colorful contact paper
- scissors

How to Make It

1. Cover the sides of selected containers with contact paper. Consider using containers such as stationery boxes, shoe boxes, or plastic storage box lids that are 1½ inches to 2 inches deep.

2. Select three to six rubber bands of different thicknesses and stretch them around the longer dimension of the container. Arrange them in sequence from thin to thick (high to low sounds).

Beautiful Beans—
Nutritious Beans

☀ Say-Along ☀

First make them a feast for the eyes
With each layer just the right size,
Then make them into a feast for the
    tummy
My, oh my, those beans are yummy!

Who: Older preschoolers and schoolagers

How to Use It
Layering beans in a clear container is a wonderful way for children to manipulate materials into a design. For children who are working on following spatial directions, you might set out an example of a completed jar. When done as a creative project, however, briefly show an example, then put it away and encourage the children to make up their own designs—there are no right or wrong ways.

Children may compare how they layered their beans differently from someone else or where they layered them in the same order. Enhance the discussion by noting, "I see you and Tara both began with a layer of kidney beans and put a layer of black-eyed peas on top. Did you layer any of the other beans or legumes the same way?" For **schoolagers** who can read, label the beans and legumes, then give them a list of the order they should place them in. Have labeled pictures available for them for basic research. They may also help you or their parents prepare a soup using the beans.

What It Does
This activity helps children become aware of design in nature and how food can be enjoyed on different levels. They will learn the characteristics of one of the major food staples in the world. The activity will enhance language development, number skills, and the ability to follow directions. When the children make the soup, they will learn about the importance of preparation (learning to anticipate) and delayed gratification (waiting for the soup to finish cooking). The Beautiful Beans Jar makes a very nice family gift.

What You Need

For the Beautiful Beans Jar:

- clear plastic jar with lid (one jar per child)
- a variety of beans (⅓ cup of each per child)
- ⅓ cup measures

To Make Eight-Bean Soup:

- 8 quart saucepan
- large bowl
- paring knife
- vegetable brush
- measuring cups

How to Make It

1. Have children clean and remove the labels from their jars. Dry thoroughly.

2. Pour beans into individual containers or roll sides of a bag down for easy access by children. Consider using lentils, dried lima beans, black beans, white beans, kidney beans, and black-eyed peas. Community co-ops are generally the most inexpensive source of beans. Put the containers of beans and measuring cups on a worktable.

3. Invite children to scoop one type of bean into the measuring cup, then empty the cup into the jar. Have them repeat the process, using beans in any order they choose.

4. Cover the jar with its lid. Let the jars grace the room with their beauty for a while, then either make soup or send the beans and the following recipe home with the children. Encourage parents and children to make the soup.

Eight-Bean Soup

⅓ cup each of dried lima beans, black beans, white beans,
    kidney beans, and black-eyed peas
½ cup each of lentils, yellow split peas, green split peas, and
    barley
3 quarts cold water
1 large chopped onion
3 large carrots
3 stalks celery with leaves, chopped
1 bay leaf
A few grains crushed red pepper (optional)
1 28 oz. can Italian plum tomatoes with juice, chopped
2 tablespoons chopped fresh basil, or 1½ teaspoons dried and
    crushed basil
salt and pepper to taste

Place all the beans together and wash them thoroughly. Add
water to cover them and soak overnight. Drain well. Add the
beans and 3 quarts of fresh water to an 8-quart saucepan.

Add the onion, carrots, celery, bay leaf, and red pepper (if
desired) to the beans. Bring to a boil. Simmer for 2 hours or
until beans are almost soft.

Add the tomatoes and cook until beans are well done.
Add the basil, salt, and pepper just before serving.

Binoculars

Who: Preschoolers and schoolagers

How to Use It

Children take the binoculars along on outdoor walks and use them to pretend to study or look at things in the distance, just as people do with real binoculars. Talk about where and how people use binoculars—such as on safari, for bird watching, or at sporting events and the opera—and encourage children to create some of these situations in dramatic play. Older children can make the binoculars themselves with a little adult assistance.

What It Does

This activity helps children become more aware of how they use their eyes. Because the binoculars screen out the periphery, they are especially useful in showing how to focus on a particular object. Using the binoculars enhances dramatic play and encourages language development through discussion of topics related to the play activity (for example, pretending to be on a safari and thinking about things to take and what will be seen).

Making binoculars encourages the development of small-motor skills and illustrates a creative use of recyclable materials.

What You Need

- toilet paper tubes (2 tubes per binoculars)
- thin ribbon, elastic, or shoelaces (about 2 to 2½ feet long)
- contact paper or construction paper (2 5- x 6-inch pieces per binoculars)
- tape
- stapler
- hole punch

How to Make It

1. Cover each tube with the paper. Cut the pieces of paper slightly larger than the tubes to allow for thorough coverage and easy taping. Staple the tubes together at the top and bottom.

2. Punch holes on the outer sides of the toilet paper tubes, about 1 inch from the top. Thread the ribbon, elastic, or shoelaces through the holes for a neck band. To secure the neck band, tie a knot at both ends so it can't slip out through the holes or staple it to each side.

❋ Say-Along ❋

My grandma has binoculars that look like these
She's always using them to look up at trees,
She tells me they help her watch the birds
And then says "warbler" and such words

Which are names of birds she sees
Sitting on branches in the trees,
Then she keeps checking in a book
And tells me to have a look.

I use my binoculars to look around
At lots of bugs on the ground,
Or when we all pretend to be
In Africa on a safari.

Gas Pump

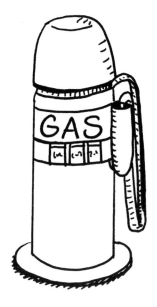

☀ Say-Along ☀

See the gas pumps all in a row
Watch the cars as they come and go,
Drive to the pump to fill up your tank
Pull down the hose and give it a crank,
When you're done put the hose in
    its slot
And remember to pay for what you got.

Who: Preschoolers and schoolagers

How to Use It
This is an excellent "make-it" project for **older preschoolers** and **schoolagers**. Collect several toothpaste pumps and ask children to think of things to make from them (for example, rockets or silos). Show the materials for making a gas pump, as well. Discuss ways of attaching the parts. Let the children make the things they would like. Encourage them to help one another, and assist as needed. Use the children's creations in the block corner when building cities and roads. The gas pumps can also be used with small cars to "fill 'er up!"

What It Does
This activity provides children with something they can make to use in their play. Use in connection with a field trip to a service station or in studying about transportation. It can also stimulate ideas for block building. Constructing the pumps uses small-motor skills and provides practice in planning and following directions. It offers an example of transforming common objects into props to use in imaginative play.

What You Need
- pump toothpaste container
- construction paper
- scissors
- cap from a pen
- shoelace
- glue stick
- cellophane tape
- marker

How to Make It

1. Cut pieces of construction paper to fit around the tooth-paste pump, allowing overlap for easy gluing. Wrap paper around the pump and glue in place.

2. Attach the pen cap just above the middle of the pump by running tape around the pump and through the plastic or metal clip on the cap. Be sure the cap opening faces up.

3. Cut the shoelace in half (so it is 12 to 14 inches in length) and tape to the pump above the pen cap. Again, run the tape around the pump and the cut end of the lace.

4. Decorate the pump with markers. Print the word *gas* and draw dials and numbers on the pump. Affix the tip of the shoelace to the pen cap.

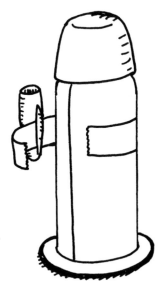

Variation

Make larger gas pumps using thin, tall cartons, thin plastic tubing for the hose, and handles from pump spray bottles. You can use a plastic or paper cup with a handle to hold the nozzle. Attach all parts with duct tape.

Furry Animals/3-D Friends

❋ Say-Along ❋

I made this Pooh-Bear for my brother
It's soft and furry as can be,
Now I think I'll make another—
A Star Trek figure just for me.

I can't believe how real they look
Or how easy they are to make,
They're just like their pictures in this
    book
And guess what—they will not break.

Who: Preschoolers and schoolagers

How to Use It
Schoolagers can make these play figures and use them as gifts for siblings, friends, or themselves. You can also use them as props in dramatic play (for example, use several bears to have a Teddy Bears' Picnic or act out the Three Bears story or other favorite bear tales). Each child can have one as a nap toy or to take home and keep. You can make other familiar characters to use in play, from other animal friends to storybook or superhero figures. Encourage children to make up their own adventures and use the characters to act them out.

What It Does
These play figures give each child a homemade replica of a favorite stuffed animal or 3-D toy. They are ideal to give to the children as holiday or end-of-the-year gifts. Parents can get involved by collecting materials for the stuffed animals (such as magazine or catalog pictures), and you can provide them with instructions on how to make the play figures.

This activity serves as a good model of making and using homemade toys. Dramatic play and acting out stories encourages language development and pre-reading and pre-writing skills. Making the toys uses small-motor skills and encourages creativity and imaginative play.

What You Need
- a picture (about 8½ x 11 inches)
- scissors
- clear contact paper
- material for the back of the figure (such as fake fur for animals, shiny plastic or oilcloth for 3-D figures)
- a plastic bag approximately the same size as the picture
- cotton batting or foam pieces
- stapler

How to Make It

1. Cut out a picture of a favorite animal toy,
   storybook or TV character. Place the contact
   paper sticky-side up on a flat surface. Center the picture
   face down on the contact paper and press to smooth. Trim
   the edges with scissors. The picture should be completely
   covered.

2. Place the animal figure on the fake fur (fur side down),
   trace around it, and cut it out. Place other characters on oilcloth or plastic in the same way.

3. Stuff cotton batting or foam pieces into the plastic bag. Fill
   to approximately 1½ inches thick. (Putting the stuffing in a
   plastic bag makes the assembly process much easier.)

4. Put the three pieces together: animal picture on one side,
   fur cutout (fur side out) on the other, stuffed bag in the
   middle. Staple or sew around the edges. If the toy is for
   toddlers, punch holes around the animal and lace or sew
   shut (toddlers can pull out staples). Schoolagers, however,
   enjoy and will be more successful with the stapler.

Quick and Easy Doll Clothes

❋ Say-Along ❋

Here is my dolly
Her name is Molly,
I've made her lots of clothes
Just like this outfit I chose.

Her shorts are red, her shirt is blue
And I think I'll make her hat red too,
Now I'll change her quick as a wink
I think I'll dress her all in pink.

It's so much fun to dress up Molly
Now let's make clothes for her sister
  Polly,
And for her baby brother Wally.

Who: Preschoolers and schoolagers

How to Use It
Children can use the clothes for dressing and undressing dolls. Have the children practice mixing and matching outfits made from various colored socks. The socks are easy for the children to pull on and off because they stretch and no buttons are involved. Children also like to wash the clothes and use clothespins to hang them on lines to dry.

Schoolagers can make the clothes themselves, decorating them with bits of lace, glitter, appliqué, or other types of designs. Make various sized clothes by using a variety of sock sizes. The socks really stretch, so even small socks can make usable outfits for small dolls.

What It Does
These doll clothes provide practice in pulling clothes on and off and fitting arms and legs into appropriate holes. The clothes also teach how to dress and undress a doll. The clothes provide an opportunity to discuss the steps involved in dressing as well as the different colors, patterns, and combinations of available clothes. Teach about the care of clothes, such as washing and folding them. Decorating the clothes develops small-motor skills and provides practice in design.

What You Need
- socks
- scissors
- needle and thread
- decorations (such as fabric paint, lace, and appliqués)
- fabric glue

How to Make It

1. Cut a sock into thirds, separating the toe section, the middle heel portion, and the top.
2. Use the top of the sock for a dress or shirt. Cut out arm holes on either side.
3. Use the midsection for shorts or pants. Sew a small closing in the middle of one end to provide the separation for legs. To create long pants, cut an arch shape in one end and sew the edges closed.
4. Fold up the edges of the toe section to make a hat.
5. Decorate as desired.

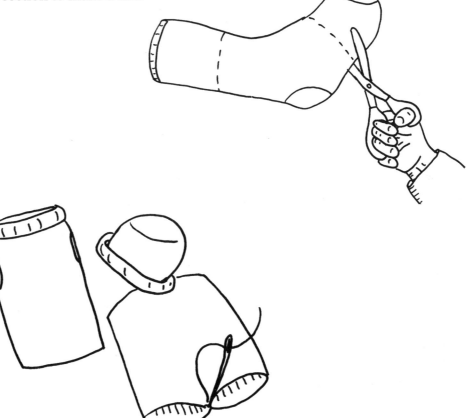

Take-Apart People

❋ Say-Along ❋

These are dolls we can put together
And dress up for any kind of weather,
Today is kind of cool and wet
So a raincoat would be a good bet,
Tomorrow whatever the weather will be
We'll dress them up accordingly.

There are lots of things these dolls can do
Their arms can move and their legs can
   too,
They can be astronauts dressed for space
Or jockeys about to enter a race,
Sometimes it's hard to fit clothes just
   right
But at least they'll never get too tight.

Who: Preschoolers and schoolagers

How to Use It

Children take the dolls apart and put them
together. Older children will be challenged
by fitting the dolls together and manipulating the fasteners.

Demonstrate how to assemble the doll and call attention
to the way the feet and hands are attached when the doll is
assembled correctly. Have the children look at their own
hands and feet and notice where their thumbs and toes point.

Older children may want to cut out or make doll clothes.
For younger children, attach Velcro to dolls and clothes for
easy changes. Use the doll in connection with other topics by
changing its outfits.

What It Does

These dolls teach recognition and awareness of body parts
and their appropriate placement. They also encourage language development through talking about ideas and words
associated with self, such as names of body parts (for
example, shaking head, waving arms, kicking feet). The dolls
encourage the development of small-motor coordination
through putting them together and taking them apart, as well
as dressing, moving, and playing with them.

Make heads with different facial expressions and use them
to talk about feelings. Dressing dolls for various occupations
expands children's knowledge of the world and provides an
opportunity to talk about what people do and how their
clothes help with their jobs.

What You Need

- patterns for arms, legs, torso, head, and wigs
- tagboard
- pencil
- markers
- scissors
- clear contact paper
- Velcro
- hole punch
- brass fasteners, ties from baggies, or Velcro
- material for doll clothes (such as fabric, colored plastic, or wallpaper samples)
- shoe box or resealable plastic bags

How to Make It

1. Trace patterns on tagboard for torso and limbs. Make your own patterns or use patterns from paper doll books.

2. Show cultural diversity by making a variety of hair types and styles and coloring the dolls in various skin tones. Show several different expressions on a number of heads. Cover with contact paper and cut out all of the parts. Add a small piece of Velcro to the top of the head and back of the hair samples.

3. Punch holes in the body parts. Use fasteners or ties to attach the limbs and head to the torso. (Velcro is better to use for younger children, but it doesn't allow for body parts to move.)

4. Make a variety of doll clothes for various occupations, seasons, and activities. Punch holes in the clothes so they fit over the brass fasteners, or attach Velcro to the doll and clothes. Store dolls and outfits in shoe boxes or resealable plastic bags.

Puzzlemania

☀ Say-Along ☀

Here's a puzzle that we can make
And it uses junk for goodness sake,
Like old candles, clips, or decoration for
a cake
And all those plastic things that are fake.

We looked inside a kitchen drawer
And found some stuff to use some more,
We took the things that we had found
And drew their shapes by tracing around.

Now its fun to try and see
Which shape each thing might be,
The outline always looks flat to me
Not like the things in reality.

(or: Not like things look in 3-D.)

How to Use It

Create instant puzzles using found objects of all sorts. Place the outline master playing board and the items that go with it on a table and let the children find the pieces that fit into the individual outlines.

Schoolagers will enjoy tracing around the objects to make these puzzles. Encourage the children to notice what the outline of an item looks like. See if they can identify the item by looking at the outline before trying the pieces. Notice that some things with irregular or specific shapes (such as a paper clip or a fork) are easy to identify while a square shape could be many different items.

With older children, discuss the concept of two-dimensional (the outline) and three-dimensional (the real object) and how that affects what things look like.

What It Does

This puzzle provides an easy-to-make activity that creatively reuses readily available materials. This, in turn, encourages the children to think about using commercial toys to create new games. The puzzle also introduces the concept of spatial relations by calling attention to shape as a tool in working a puzzle. It also sharpens visual-perception and small-motor skills.

What You Need

- tagboard
- assortment of objects with differing shapes
- markers
- clear contact paper
- container
- Velcro

How to Make It

1. Select six to eight clean objects. Consider using cookie cutters, plastic silverware, block shapes, small toys, discarded puzzle pieces, keys, rubber bands, chalk, or old combs.
2. Trace around each shape on the tagboard. Use a 12- x 18-inch piece of tagboard for larger puzzles.
3. Cover the tagboard with contact paper. Place the objects in a container. When making multiple puzzles, color code the back of the tagboard and the container of objects that go with it.

Variations

For portable puzzles, trace the objects on a box top (such as a stationery or candy box) or mount tagboard on a box top. Keep matching objects in the box. For a traveling puzzle, attach Velcro to the objects and to the matching spot on the outline on the box lid.

To make an outdoor version of this puzzle, use chalk to trace objects (such as leaves, rocks, branches, or plants) on the sidewalk.

To make an indoor version, use oilcloth or vinyl place mats and washable markers or crayons to trace a collection of objects. Children match the objects to the outlines and then wipe off the mat and start again with different objects.

Moving Target Toss

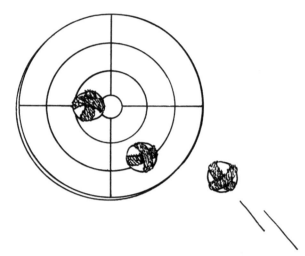

☀ Say-Along ☀

Watch me toss this little ball
It sticks to you and doesn't fall,
Twist it off and play some more
We will count to keep the score.

Playing this game is lots of fun
We try to hit targets as they run,
But one thing we've learned is this:
Usually we toss and miss!

Who: Preschool and schoolagers

How to Use It

Target vests can be worn by children, adults, or draped over chairs or low library racks. Demonstrate tossing balls gently at vests or wall targets. Explain how easily the ball sticks with a light toss and the best place to aim (the mid area). Show how to remove the balls by twisting them.

Younger children will just use the targets to attach and detach the balls. **Older preschoolers** and **schoolagers** will enjoy playing simple dodgeball-type games with some children wearing vests and others tossing the balls at the moving targets. Make up rules for the games. For example, when a player's "target" is hit, that player sits down or exchanges place with the child who threw the ball. Devise a point system and change teams when so many points are scored by the tossing team.

Mount stationary targets on walls, either indoors or out. Use Velcro patches for easy relocation. These targets can be used by individual children or by small teams playing a game.

What It Does

This activity provides an opportunity for children to follow directions and successfully participate in a simple nonthreatening game. It helps children develop visual-motor skills in an active way without fear of failing or being hurt. The activity strengthens hand-eye coordination and throwing skills. Children learn to watch the ball as it moves in space, and often they move their hands toward it as it reaches their vest.

For older children, this activity provides practice in making up games and following procedures. Devising and using a scoring system provides practice in counting and using numbers.

What You Need

- fabric for vest
- 1½-inch strapping fabric or elastic
- scissors
- needle and thread or fabric glue
- Velcro strips
- Nerf balls or old socks

How to Make It

1. For each vest cut two 10- x 14-inch fabric panels and four 8-inch lengths of strapping fabric or elastic. For the fabric panels, consider using Velcro fabric, flannel-backed vinyl, or nubby wool or jersey fabrics.

2. Sew or glue two lengths of strapping fabric to the top of each panel along the 10-inch edge, leaving about 6 inches between the straps for child's head. Attach the remaining two straps to the side of the back panel, about 8 inches down from the top of the vest. Attach a piece of Velcro to the inside of the other ends so that the user can secure it to the front panel.

3. Make fabric balls from old socks rolled up and wadded inside themselves. Wrap 1½- to 2-inch lengths of Velcro around the fabric balls or other small balls. (Test to make sure Velcro sticks to fabric vest.)

Variation

Create a number game with the vests. Mount numerals on several vests and have children toss or place the corresponding number of balls on each vest.

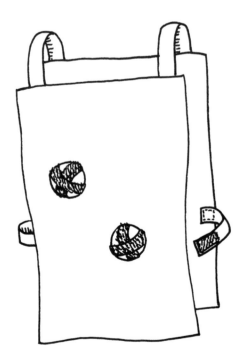

Sizzling Rockets

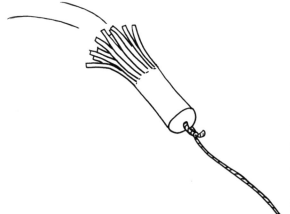

Who: Preschoolers and schoolagers

How to Use It

Assemble the materials and assist children as needed. **Older preschoolers** and **schoolagers** can make these as a craft activity related to learning about rockets or for experimenting with air, motion, and flight. Children can whirl them around in the air (inside or outside) and watch their rockets sparkle and flash their sizzling tails as they whirl around.

Children can also launch their rockets by slipping them over a thin tube, dowel, or ruler and making a motion similar to an overhand throw. The rocket will fly off the launching device, traveling several yards before landing. It is best to launch the rockets outside or in a gym, where children can practice seeing how far their rockets will go.

What It Does

These rockets provide a fun craft activity to make and use in a unit on rockets. Building the rockets provides practice in small-motor and hand-eye coordination, following directions, and completing a task. It encourages talking about rockets and discussing parts, construction, shape, and appearance. It provides an opportunity to observe how air affects the rocket as it moves through the air.

Playing with the rockets provides practice in running and throwing, two basic large-motor skills preschool children need to develop. Making up ways to play with the rocket encourages creativity. Running and flying the rocket develops coordination.

❋ Say-Along ❋

I'd like to blast off in a rocket ship
And go orbiting out in space,
On a whirling, swirling trip
To a very far-off place.

We can stop at the space station
As we head to the moon,
Just use your imagination
But be sure to come back soon.

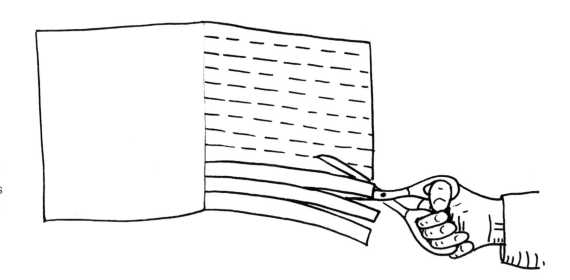

What You Need

- toilet paper tubes
- shiny Mylar, 6- x 10-inch pieces
- scissors
- cellophane tape
- hole punch
- string cut into 2- to 2½-foot pieces
- thin cardboard tubes (such as from plastic wrap, dowels, round pillar type blocks, or rulers) to use as launchers

How to Make It

1. Fold the Mylar paper in half lengthwise. Open and fringe one half, making cuts about half an inch apart and 5 inches long (to the fold line).

2. Cover the toilet paper tubes with the Mylar so one end is flush with the end of the tube and the fringe extends beyond the other end. Secure with tape.

3. Punch a hole approximately 1 inch from the unfringed end of the tube. Loop the string through the hole and tie. (You may staple the string to the tube, but you should also tie a knot in the string to prevent it from slipping through the staples.)

4. Hold the end of the string and whirl the tube around, turning and twisting it for added motion and effect. Children can launch their rockets by slipping them over a thin tube, dowel, or ruler and making a motion similar to an overhand throw.

Puzzle Fix-It

❋ Say-Along ❋

For puzzles that are made of wood
This way to fix 'em is very good:
You mix the putty just like clay
Then shape the piece in a special way,
Sand it and paint it and when it's through
The puzzle will almost be good as new.

Who: Preschoolers and schoolagers

How to Use It

This technique encourages **schoolagers** to care for and repair materials by giving them an opportunity to make and replace lost puzzles pieces. Demonstrate the process of mixing the wood putty, lining the empty puzzle space with plastic wrap, and filling it in with wood putty. Discuss what can be done when the piece dries (such as sanding the edges and painting or coloring the piece to match the puzzle). Use this activity in a dramatic play fix-it shop.

    Schoolagers will be able to do this on their own after some demonstration and with some supervision. **Preschoolers** can assist in phases of the process, such as sanding and painting.

What It Does

This activity helps save money by providing a way to extend the usefulness of puzzles after a piece has been lost. It teaches about care, maintenance, and repair of materials and facilitates discussion about when something can be repaired. The activity encourages the development of repair skills as well as feelings of accomplishment. It encourages planning, following directions, and problem-solving skills (how to make the piece look right for the puzzle).

What You Need
- puzzles with missing pieces
- wood putty
- plastic wrap
- acrylic paints
- small paintbrushes
- medium grade sandpaper
- spoon

How to Make It

1. Complete the puzzle. Line the opening where the puzzle piece is missing with plastic wrap. Allow the plastic wrap to overlap an inch or more on all sides of the opening.

2. Fill the plastic-lined opening with putty so that the putty fits completely around all of the sides and is level with the rest of the puzzle.

3. Let the putty dry completely (usually 24 hours). When it is dry, lift it up by the edges of the plastic wrap and remove the dried piece.

4. Sand the edges of the piece that feel uneven or do not fit smoothly. Paint the piece to match the puzzle.

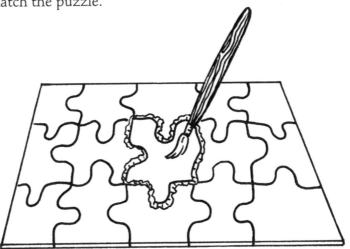

The Desert in a Peanut Butter Jar

☀ Say-Along ☀

I bet that you did not know
Even in sand some things can grow;
One such thing is called a "cactus"
And in the desert they get lots of practice.

Cactus plants come in different kinds
But they all have sharp and prickly spines,
They do not need much water to grow
As my desert garden in this jar will show.

Who: Preschoolers and schoolagers

How to Use It
Preschoolers and **schoolagers** alike will enjoy taking part in creating a desert environment in a peanut butter jar. Children can help collect sand and rocks for the terrarium.

Encourage children to observe how cacti and other desert plants are different from most houseplants. Wonder with the children why cacti are so prickly, how big they grow, and whether or not any animals like to eat them. View videos on cacti and the desert and learn the answers.

When the children have completed their desert gardens and their study of desert plants, they can give the gardens to their parents and impress them with their knowledge.

What It Does
This activity introduces children to some of the wonders of the desert environment and helps all children gain an understanding and appreciation of differences in nature. It teaches observation skills and promotes language development.

What You Need
- jar
- sand
- small rocks
- small cactus plants
- tongs
- hammer and nail

How to Make It

1. Wash and remove the label from a jar. Any large, wide-mouthed, plastic jar with a lid will work (glass jars will work, but plastic is safer). Add 2 to 3 inches of sand to the bottom of the jar. Using tongs, make shallow dents in the sand where the cactus plants will be placed.

2. With tongs, carefully place the cacti into the dents. Drop in some small rocks. Arrange the rocks with tongs, if necessary.

3. Sprinkle just enough water into the jar to wet the sand. For continuing care, add water *only* when no beads of water moisture can be seen on the inside of the jar.

4. Make small holes in the lid with the hammer and nail. Screw the lid onto the jar.

Do-Able

A good book to read is *Walk in the Desert*, by Caroline Arnold (Silver Burdett, 1990), which has beautiful pictures of plants and animals that live in the desert. Its simple text vividly describes the conditions found in a desert environment.

Hanging Planter

How to Use It

Children can help fill these planters with dirt, learn how to plant seeds or how to transplant seedlings, and how to care for the plants. Younger children can learn to observe how plants grow, such as how they grow toward the light. **Older schoolagers** might do some simple experiments, such as noting how different amounts of water or light can affect how the plants thrive. This can lead to discussions on the importance of rain during growing seasons.

Children can braid yarn for hanging the planter or make Styrofoam bases for keeping the planters stable on a windowsill.

What It Does

This activity results in an attractive planter that you can add to a science area to help teach about the care of plants and how certain aspects of weather affect crops that farmers grow. Small planters would make nice gifts for family members.

What You Need

- plastic soda pop bottles with caps
- marker
- knife or scissors
- yarn
- potting soil
- crushed rock
- seeds or small plants
- Styrofoam meat tray, 1 to 2 inches deep

☀ Say-Along ☀

Oh, do you know what makes plants
    grow?
What makes plants grow, what makes
    plants grow?
Oh, do you know what makes plants
    grow?
This is what I know!

Water and light helps them grow
Helps them grow, helps them grow,
Water and light helps make them grow
So, water them just so.

(*Sing to the tune of "Do You Know the
Muffin Man?" as a round or a question
and answer.*)

How to Make It

1. Place the bottle on its side and draw a rectangle shape in the center. Using the knife or scissors, cut out a large opening along the lines.

2. Poke holes through the bottle, one on each short side of the opening (holes should be directly across from one another). Braid yarn and thread it through the holes. Tie large knots on each end of the yarn to secure it to the bottle.

3. Fill the bottom of the planter with crushed rock for drainage. Add dirt and sow seeds according to package directions or plant small plants. Place the planter in a well-lit area and water judiciously.

4. To create a stand for placing the planter on a windowsill, turn over the Styrofoam tray and cut an oval hole down the center. This oval hole will support the middle section of the bottle. Place the planter into the stand.

Do-Able

Read *Seeds and More Seeds,* by Millicent Selsam (Harper, 1959), and have the children try some of the experiments it suggests or use similar stories to help provide ideas for experimenting with factors that affect how plants grow.

Pulleys for Work and Play

☀ Say-Along ☀

To make a pulley here's the deal:
You need something round like a wheel
For a rope to go over and turn it around
To pull the load up off the ground.

Pulleys are very useful to us
They lift heavy loads without a fuss,
And move lots of stuff from here to
  there
You see them at work sites everywhere.

Our pulleys are really lots of fun
We can lift up these animals one by one,
Making them go up and down is neat
When we're done we tie it to a cleat.

Who: Preschoolers and Schoolagers

How to Use It

To introduce children to the use of the wheel, one of the three basic machines (a lever and the inclined plane are the other two), make a simple homemade pulley toy out of things from around the house or purchase pulleys at a hardware store. Use the pulleys to create a working system for such things as raising and lowering a hammock full of soft toys, moving a birdfeeder between a tree and a window, or hauling buckets of water to the sandbox.

Schoolagers can gather the materials needed to make the simple pulleys and can help in their construction. They can also help figure out how to raise and lower a hammock or other storage container using several pulleys and some clothesline.

Explain to **preschoolers** that pulleys are just wheels that help make lifting and moving things easier. Pulleys, for example, help make our cars run and make it possible to lift heavy steel beams to the top of tall buildings. Ask the children if they know of any other ways pulleys are working in their environment (for example, venetian blinds or elevators).

What It Does

Pulleys introduce children to another way to use wheels. They help children learn about physics through hands-on experience. This activity promotes language development as you and the children discuss components of pulleys, how they work, and the different ways people can use them. Pulleys encourage schoolagers to use their imaginations as they figure out different uses for them, and they promote large- and small-motor coordination, problem-solving skills, and experimenting with scientific thinking.

There are two options for this activity—homemade pulleys and working pulleys. The homemade pulley will not support much weight, but it can be used much like a clothesline for drying paintings or doll clothes or to support a basket for messages or other small, light items. In this system, two homemade pulleys are used at either end of a continuous loop of rope. The second option, working pulleys, requires store-bought pulleys, which can support more weight. One working pulley can be set up very simply, with a bucket or basket on one end of the rope, to raise or lower toys from a loft, for example. Two working pulleys can be used in the same clothesline-type system as the homemade ones—that is, at either end of a continuous loop of rope—and used to move heavier items like a bird feeder or buckets of sand or water outside. Or three pulleys can be set up to raise and lower a hammock or net full of soft toys, as in the example below.

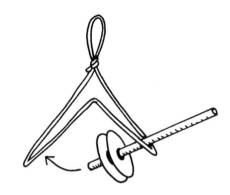

Homemade Pulleys: What You Need
- 2 heavy-duty wire clothes hangers
- 2 empty metal or plastic adhesive tape reels (such as those used for medical purposes)
- glue
- pliers
- 2½-inch-diameter dowels (each 12 to 15 inches long)
- rope
- 4 rubber bands
- ice cream bucket
- clothespins (for hanging doll clothes or paintings)

Homemade Pulleys: How to Make It
1. Bend up the bottom of the hanger to form an upside down V shape. With the pliers, bend the hook of the hanger to make a closed loop.

2. Lay the dowel into one curve or "arm" of the hanger. Slip the reel onto the dowel, then lay the dowel into the other curve or "arm" so each end rests in one "arm" of the hanger.

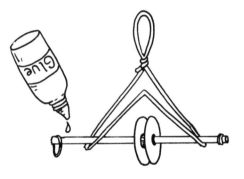

3. Place a rubber band on each end of the dowel near the hanger and apply glue (this keeps the dowel from slipping off the hanger). Make a second pulley in the same way.

4. Suspend the hangers at the same height and far enough apart that children can see the pulley action. If you want a temporary clothesline, you could hang one end on a door-knob and the other on the back of a chair, for example.

5. Measure a straight line from one of the reels to the other to determine how far apart they are. Cut a piece of rope or clothesline twice that distance plus a foot.

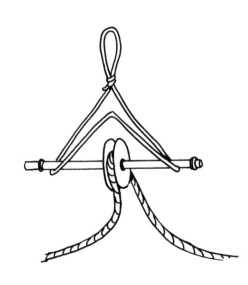

6. If you want an ice cream bucket or a basket on the line for sending messages or small items, tie it in the middle of the line.

7. Feed the rope around both reels, pull it snug, and tie the ends together to form a continuous loop. If you've tied a basket onto the rope, make sure the basket is on the bottom of the loop. If you're going to use the line for hanging doll clothes or paintings, add clothespins.

Working Pulley System: What You Need

- two 1-inch pulleys, one single and one double (a double pulley has two wheels and can accommodate two ropes)
- 1 cleat
- rope or clothesline
- 2 hooks
- doll-sized hammock or net

Working Pulley System: How to Make It

1. Measure the length of the hammock. Attach two hooks to the ceiling or high up on the wall the same distance apart as the length of the hammock. Be sure the hooks are anchored into studs or joists so they will be strong enough to hold the weight of the hammock.

2. Fasten a cleat to a wall directly below or in line with one of the hooks. Make sure the cleat is within the children's reach.

3. Hang the double pulley on the hook above the cleat. Hang the single pulley on the other hook.

4. Measure two lengths of rope. The length of the first rope has to be twice the distance from the floor to the pulley. The length of the second rope must be twice the distance from the floor to the pulley plus the distance between the two pulleys.

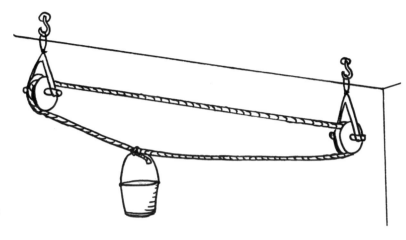

5. Lay the hammock on the floor. Tie the shorter rope to one end of the hammock and the longer rope to the other end. Thread the shorter rope through one side of the double pulley. Thread the longer rope over the single pulley and then through the other wheel of the double pulley. (See the diagram below.)

6. Show the children how to pull on both ropes at once to raise the hammock evenly and as high as they want it. Let them experiment with what happens if they pull only one rope, or if they pull one rope faster than the other. Show them how to wrap the rope in a figure eight around the cleat to keep the hammock in place.

Do-Able

Pulleys, by Michael Dahl (Capstone Press, 1998) has an excellent explanation of pulleys and wonderful illustrations of them at work on flagpoles, cranes, ski lifts, and drawbridges. It also has a bibliography of other books to look at for more information.

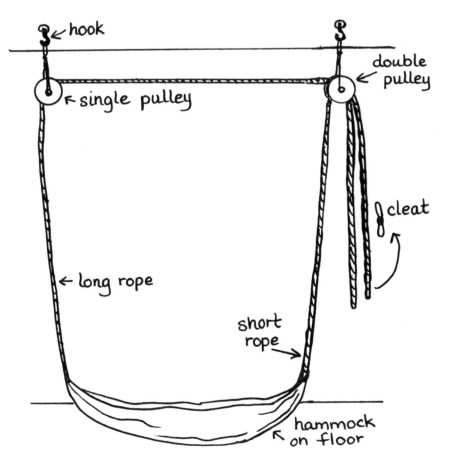

VI.
All Ages

Child-Safe Display Rack

❋ Say-Along ❋

Hang your picture up so high
Leave it awhile so it can dry,
All the bright colors on the wall
Carefully hung so they won't fall.

Push the clothespin—that's the trick
Slide in the picture and let it go—click,
Now your picture is right in place
It looks just like a smiling face.

Who: All ages

How to Use It

Use this display rack to dry or display children's artwork. Older children can hang their own pictures or pictures they have cut from magazines or calendars. They can also use the rack to arrange pictures in a sequence to tell a story about something they have done or learned about or to classify and place them into like-groups or pairs.

Hang up pictures of faces and design patterns for **infants** to look at. Display pictures of everyday objects for **toddlers** and **young preschoolers** to identify. You can also use this display rack as a mitten rack, smock holder, or message holder.

What It Does

This display rack provides an easy, safe, and manageable way for children to display things and change them when desired. The rack encourages independence, self-sufficiency, and hand-eye coordination as the children hang and take down pictures at will. It also promotes language development, logical thinking, and sequencing skills when used for discussion of pictures or picture stories.

What You Need
- 1- x 2-inch pine board
- sandpaper
- spring-type clothespins (2 per foot of board)
- hammer and finishing nails
- hand drill
- pencil
- ruler
- wood glue

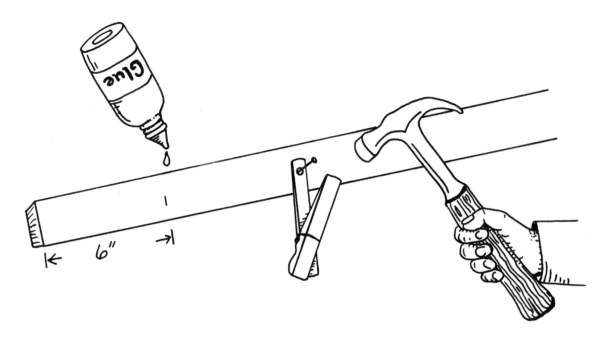

How to Make It

1. Cut the board to desired length and sand smooth. Measure and mark off 6-inch intervals along the board.

2. Twist clothespins apart slightly and drill a small hole about ½ to ¾ inch from the top of one-half of the clothespin. (If clothespins should come apart, put them back together by snapping each half around the spring.)

3. Place a small dab of glue below the hole on the back of the clothespin. Place each clothespin at the designated marks.

4. Hammer a nail through each hole to attach the clothespins to the board. Snap clothespin into place. Press to secure the glue.

Note: Attach the display rack firmly to the wall at the children's level for a permanent display board. Or you can use it as a moveable drying rack where needed (for example, over a bathtub or laundry tub to dry doll clothes or between two chairs to hang mittens or special projects).

Variations

For a quick and easy display system, attach half of a Velcro patch to the side of the clothespins. Stick the other half of the patch to a wall or large board at the children's level. The clothespins will stick to the patches and can be used to hang items as discussed above.

You can also use this variation at an adult level in prominent places to clip notes as reminders to staff, parents, or yourself.

Milk Carton Puppets

Who: All ages

How to Use It

These wonderful puppets lend a special excitement to the telling of familiar stories and nursery rhymes. Bears, bunnies, kittens, puppies, and lambs are particularly useful puppets to have around. Children can use small milk cartons (such as pints) to help dramatize their imaginative play as they delve into space or pretend to be firefighters. **Infants** and **toddlers** will simply enjoy having you make animal sounds, using the puppet as a prop, during interaction time. **Toddlers** and **preschoolers** will especially like using the puppets with stories and rhymes. **Older preschoolers** and **school-agers** can put on a puppet show for their parents or the younger children. They can take part in planning which puppets are needed, and then they can help construct them.

What It Does

Puppets encourage children to tell stories, which develops language and memory skills. Often children who are shy about talking or seem to forget what they want to say are comfortable expressing themselves through a puppet. Puppets also encourage children to create original stories. All of these are skills that contribute to reading readiness and literacy and help build self-esteem.

What You Need

For each puppet:
- 1 clean paper milk carton
- pencil
- ruler
- scissors
- glue
- staples or needle and thread
- fabric and felt
- toilet paper roll

❊ Say-Along ❊

Can you believe this puppet friend
Is really a milk carton that you bend?
We made them by ourselves today
And now we can use them in our play.

Furry animals or soldiers tall
We can make them one and all,
We'll make up stories for them to tell
Or use them in tales we know so well.

How to Make It

Bunny

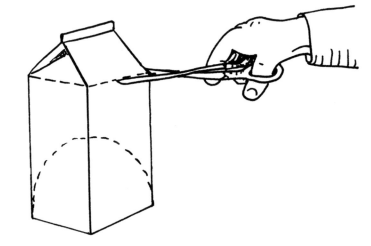

1. Cut off the top section of the milk carton. Choose a carton size that is most appropriate for the type of puppet and the hand size of the puppeteer. Thoroughly wash and dry the carton.

2. Place the carton on its bottom. Along one edge, make a mark 3 inches down from the top rim. On both sides, draw an arched line from the mark to the bottom corners. Cut along that line. Trim away curved remnants, leaving a band around the top of the carton (which will be the bottom of the puppet).

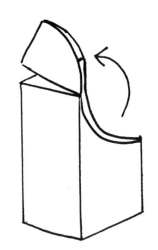

3. Turn the carton over so the bottom side is up. Cut a square of felt (the color you want for the mouth) the size of the milk carton bottom and glue it on. Fold bottom diagonally and flip the curved section up to create the mouth and the face.

4. Cut the fabric to cover the carton and glue it on. For reinforcement, staple or sew around all edges. Sew small pieces of fabric to form arms and sew or staple to main puppet.

5. Cut ears from toilet paper roll. Cut and glue felt to the inner ear and fur to the outer ear. Reinforce by sewing or stapling around each ear. Sew or staple ears to the main puppet.

6. Cut black or other felt pieces for eyes and nose. Glue on facial features and decorations.

Variations

Bear Puppet: Follow directions for Bunny through step 2, except draw in the bear's ears as you draw the arch for the head. Glue on mouth as for Bunny, then glue or sew woolly fabric onto the rest of the carton. Cut out a dark felt circle and sew it over the front corner of the face (overlap extra fabric to make it fit) and make smaller circles for eyes.

Other Puppets: Experiment with other materials and ideas to create puppets to suit your needs, using the above pattern as your basic model.

Milk Carton Blocks

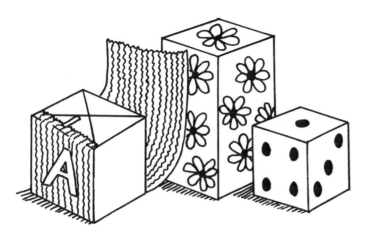

☀ Say-Along ☀

Blocks can make so many things
From roads for cars to thrones for kings!

With a little imagination
These blocks can be a station
Filled with people waiting for trains.

But now in a jiffy
I'll make it a nifty
Control tower guiding planes.

For the most fun of all
Build a tower tall
Then push it and watch it fall.

Yes, blocks can make so many things
And building makes us feel like kings!

Who: All ages

How to Use It

Infants who are learning to crawl will find small colorful blocks, placed just out of their reach, enticing objects to go for. Sitting **infants** will handle and explore the blocks. New walkers will enjoy carrying the blocks about. **Toddlers** can use small blocks for dump-and-fill activities or practice stacking a few at a time and then knocking them over. **Preschoolers** will begin using different-sized blocks for some serious building or laying them in rows for roadways for small cars. Place numbers, dots, or designs on the blocks to play counting games. **Schoolagers** can create buildings for neighborhood or city scenes by decorating different-sized blocks. For all ages, placing objects inside blocks turns them into rattles or instruments for rhythm bands.

What It Does

Blocks help develop hand-eye coordination and encourage large-motor development for infants. They encourage familiarity with shapes and sizes and problem-solving skills. Block play encourages social development. (Because milk carton blocks are so inexpensive, you can easily have enough for every child to play with—which is important for early social interaction and learning to work together.) Counting and comparing shapes and sizes promote understanding of basic word and number concepts. Using blocks as instruments helps children be a part of making music and developing their sense of rhythm.

What You Need

For each block:

- 2 milk cartons or boxes of the same size
- scissors
- newspapers
- colorful contact paper or durable paper
- tape or clear contact paper
- markers
- noise-making items

How to Make It

1. Cut the tops off each carton at the same place. (How much is cut off determines the length of the block.) Thoroughly wash and dry the cartons.

2. Slip one empty carton over the other to make a building block. For sturdier, weightier building blocks, stuff one of the bottoms with crumpled newspaper before fitting the second carton over it. (Be careful not to overstuff since that can round the sides and make building with them difficult.) If you're making a rhythm instrument, fill one carton with desired noise-making items (such as sand, pebbles, or rice) before fitting the second one over it.

3. Cover the block with colorful contact paper or wrap it like a package with sturdy paper, such as a grocery bag, and tape the ends securely.

4. If desired, use markers to draw numbers or shapes on the block. Or cut out decorations, place them on the block, and cover with clear contact paper.

Variations

Make dice for children to use with board games. Make a block with the height equal to the width, following the steps above. Cover the block with white paper and draw dots on it to resemble dice.

Make a shape sorter by cutting two cartons the same size (as previously illustrated). Cover each of the open cartons with plain contact paper. Push cartons together. Draw shapes slightly larger than the objects intended to fit through the holes. With a utility knife, cut out the designs. These blocks will challenge children to take apart the two sections of the block and then match the correct shapes when they put them back together.

Make fit-together matching cubes. Follow the directions for making the dice (see the first variation), using quart-, pint-, or cup-sized cartons. Create matching themes (number, pattern, or color) for each set of cubes. Apply half of a section of Velcro to two opposite sides of each cube, making sure that the hook and loop parts of the Velcro are attached in such a way that the child can match the cubes correctly.

The Versatile Scoop Toy

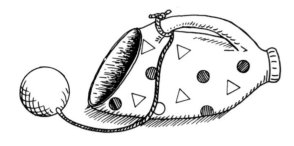

☀ Say-Along ☀

To play with this scoop
You catch things in its loop
This ball on a string
May be just the thing.

Give the ball a little fling
And scoop it up on the wing
Keep on trying to make a catch
Before you know it we'll play a match.

Who: All ages

How to Use It

Infants will study this scoop toy and explore it with their hands. They will put toys into and out of it. **Toddlers** will use it as a helmet or, with a string and pom-pom tied to it, they will use it as a pull toy. **Preschoolers** and **schoolagers** will find it challenging to use it to play catch with each other, using soft balls (such as pom-poms or a whiffle ball) or badminton birdies. One child can use the scoop as a solitary toss-and-catch game by using a string to attach a ball to the scoop. The scoop also makes a great sandbox toy.

What It Does

This scoop toy encourages infants to explore the characteristics of materials. It provides toddlers with opportunities for imaginative play as well as enhancing motor development. It encourages older children to play together and create games while also improving their hand-eye coordination and large-motor skills. The scoop toy also provides an example of using a discarded material in many fun and useful ways.

What You Need
- 2 or more bleach bottles
- scissors
- contact paper or stickers
- light, soft ball

How to Make It

1. Thoroughly wash and dry the bottles. Carefully cut each one to make a scoop. Yarn or seam binding and glue can be used to cover the cut edge of the scoop.

2. Decorate the scoop with shapes cut from contact paper, or use stickers.

Variation

For a ball and scoop game, braid a 2-foot length of yarn. Tie one end to the scoop handle and fasten a ball to the other end. The longer the string, the harder the task. For younger or less skilled children, shorten the length until they can work with it successfully.

Caution: Do not leave string on scoops if infants or very young toddlers will be using them.

Finger Puppets

Who: All ages

How to Use It
Infants will enjoy playing hide-and-seek games as you or an older child wear a finger puppet. **Toddlers** who are beginning to talk can imitate words and animal sounds, or they can wear finger puppets and carry on a conversation with puppets that you or another child is wearing. **Preschoolers** can act out stories that have been read to them. **Schoolagers** can make up their own plays using the puppets or, with some help, create the puppets for use by themselves or younger children.

What It Does
Puppets can help infants understand the existence of something even when it is out of sight (object permanence) and practice visual tracking or locate sounds (for example, a bell attached to a puppet). Puppets encourage toddlers and preschoolers to express their feelings and ideas, helping enhance their verbal skills and confidence. Puppets encourage play with others, creativity, and small-motor development. Store the puppets in a container that has been appropriately marked.

Caution: Do not let infants or toddlers handle puppets that have small objects attached to them. If these objects come loose, they could be harmful.

What You Need
- glove
- scissors
- needle and thread or fabric glue
- markers or fabric paint or bits of fabric, fringe, yarn, ribbon
- container with lid

How to Make It
1. Cut the fingers off the glove and hem or glue around the raw edge of each finger so it will not ravel.
2. Sew, glue, or paint interesting faces onto the finger sections of each glove, adding fringe or other decorations for added interest.

❋ Say-Along ❋

Hello, Mr. Puppet, (*wave to puppet*)
How are you today?
Very well, my little pet,
Would you like to play? (*wiggle puppet*)
Can you do some tricks with me?
Shake your head 1, 2, 3 (*shake head three times*)
Can you turn round and round? (*puppet and child turn*)
Now see if you can make this sound:
_____ (*have puppet make various sounds for children to repeat; use animal sounds for toddlers*)

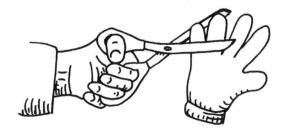

Bongo Drum

✹ Say-Along ✹

Boom, Boom, Boom
Hear the loud drum beat.
Stamp, Stamp, Stamp
Go our little busy feet.
Marching, Marching, Marching
Here we come.
Boom, Boom, Boom
To the beat of the drum.

(Use this verse as a marching activity while playing drums.)

Who: All ages

How to Use It
Infants and **toddlers** can experiment with hitting the drum to make noise. **Preschoolers** and **schoolagers** will beat on the drum while singing and playing other instruments or when listening to recorded music or expressing their own inner rhythms. They can be actively involved in making their own instrument.

What It Does
Beating on a drum helps infants and toddlers develop hand-eye coordination and upper body strength while receiving a noisy feedback from their own actions. Very satisfying! It helps preschoolers and schoolagers actively express a feel for music and rhythm and refine their listening skills while enhancing upper body strength and coordination.

What You Need

- metal can (such as a 2- or 3-pound coffee can)
- scissors
- colorful paper or contact paper
- crayons or markers
- glue
- clear contact paper
- plastic lid or piece of leather (up to 9 x 9 inches)
- string or heavy rubber band
- wooden spoon or dowel

How to Make It

1. Cut a piece of paper to fit the outside of the can. Have children draw designs on the paper with crayons or marker.

2. Glue the paper to the can. For a longer lasting drum, place clear contact paper over the decorated paper, or simply cover with colorful contact paper.

3. Place the lid on the can. If you are using a piece of leather for the drum's top, cut a circle out of the leather a few inches wider than the rim of the can. Center the circle over the open end of the can. Wrap the string or rubber band several times around the can and the overlapping edges of the leather.

4. Use the wooden spoon or dowel for drumsticks. Make sure they are smooth, splinter-free, and kid-proof.

Crawl-Through Boxes and Tunnels

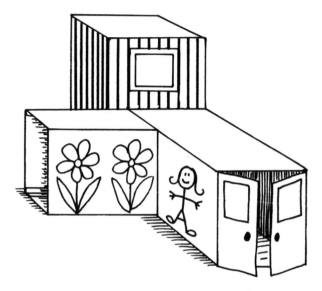

☀ Say-Along ☀

For infants:

Peek-a-boo—I see you
Look! You can crawl right through.
Creeping, Crawling—Come right here
You are such a little dear.
Creeping, Crawling—No need to hurry
Touch the sides so soft and furry.

For older children:

Tell me all the different ways
You can crawl through this maze.
Try to wiggle on your tummy
Or slide through on your back
Or pretend you are a train
running on a track.
You can go swimming like a fish
You can be anything you wish.
How does it feel with your eyes shut
    tight?
And what's at the end of the tunnel?
    Light!

Who: All ages

How to Use It
Provide a single-box tunnel for **infants** to test their crawling skills. To help **infants** work on separation anxiety, play peek-a-boo with them by popping in and out of sight at the other end. Line the inside of the crawl-through with different textures; when playing with **infants** and **toddlers**, describe how each crawl-through feels. Add extra boxes, at different angles, for **toddlers** and **preschoolers** for exciting "chase-me-in-the-maze" games or as part of indoor or outdoor obstacle courses. **Schoolagers** can make their own tunnels and mazes and use them in dramatic play (for example, tunneling under the ocean).

What It Does
The crawl-through provides infants an opportunity to safely test the use of their bodies inside a semi-confined area. It helps infants and toddlers work through separation anxiety and provides them with hands-on tactile experience and related language development. The crawl-through provides toddlers and preschoolers with large-motor development and rudimentary game-playing skills. The crawl-through provides schoolagers with an inexpensive resource that helps them learn to design and implement their own dramatic play construction.

What You Need
- sturdy cardboard boxes
- extra cardboard for reinforcing strips
- pencil
- ruler
- utility knife
- glue or tape
- carpet squares, fuzzy fabric, smooth fabric or vinyl

How to Make It

For each box:

1. Cut four pieces of cardboard 5 inches wide and the length of the box. Measure and score each piece 1-inch in from the edge of the long sides.

2. Open both ends of each box. Bend the scored parts slightly. Apply glue to the outside of the bent parts. Glue each piece into the inside corners of the box, forming a triangular brace. When dry, reinforce with tape.

3. Glue materials and fabrics to the inside of the box. If desired, cover the outside of the box with contact paper or other materials.

4. To make tunnels and mazes, reinforce as in steps 1 and 2. Add textures or decorations to fit the theme and tape boxes together.

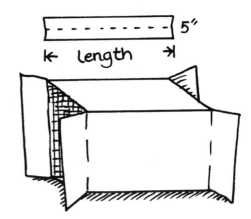

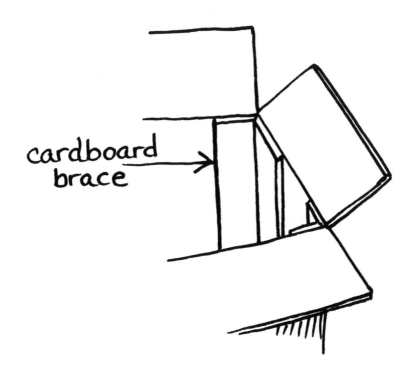

cardboard brace

Step-Up Aerobics for Kids

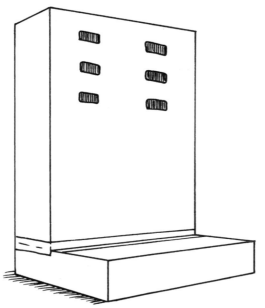

☀ Say-Along ☀

Hey, step right up here
Give it a try.
Left foot then right foot
Stepping up so high.

Just keep on moving
Fast as you can go.
Left foot then right foot
Like marching in a show.

Keep up the rhythm
Don't let it slow.
Left foot then right foot
Keep it on the go.

(Sing to the tune of "Hey, Look Me Over."
Keep repeating through workout time)

Who: All ages

How to Use It

Add this piece of inexpensive workout equipment to the large-motor area for children to use as the spirit moves them or as part of a group exercise activity. **Infants** and **young toddlers** can explore the use of their bodies by either climbing or stepping on the step-up. **Older toddlers** and **younger preschoolers** can practice stepping up and down. **Older preschoolers** and **schoolagers** may be encouraged to count as they step up and down or to practice their understanding of "right" and "left" by saying "right foot up; right foot down; left foot up; left foot down." Use the step-up with music or an exercise video. You can make it wide enough so several children can use it side by side, or you can make it four-sided for group aerobic exercise. Discuss with children how walking, running, and using the step-up helps keep their hearts healthy and strong.

What It Does

The step-up encourages children to exercise the muscles in their legs. It introduces them to the notion that using their legs not only builds strong leg muscles but also is an important part of overall aerobic health because it also benefits their lungs and heart. The step-up also helps children learn the concept of "left" and "right," practice counting, and experience the joy of using their bodies.

What You Need
- 2 sturdy cardboard boxes
- newspapers
- duct tape
- utility knife

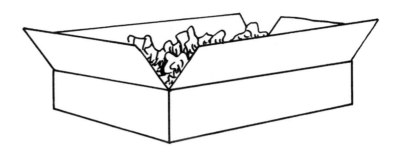

How to Make It

1. For the base, stuff crumpled newspaper into a flat cardboard box that is approximately 8 x 18 x 18 inches. Box size will vary according to the size of children using the step-up and whether or not it is intended for single or multiple use. Securely tape shut the openings.

2. For the handle, choose a tall, sturdy box that, when placed on end, is approximately 10 x 18 inches and tall enough for the tallest child in the group to hold onto comfortably. Open up one end of the box, and tape all other sides shut.

3. Lay the base box in a horizontal position. Place the tall box with the open end up, aligning one side of the tall box with the back of the base. Tape the two boxes securely together. Push the flaps of the open end inside the box for reinforcement. Cut the small openings (handles) at appropriate height for shorter children.

4. Cover both boxes with contact paper or let children decorate them with markers.

Variation

For a four-sided step-up, choose a large enough base box to allow about 8 inches on all four sides when the handle box is placed in the middle. Proceed as for single person step-up.

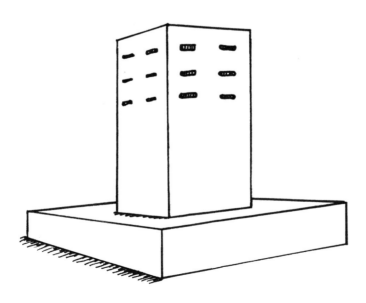

Bug Keeper

❈ Say-Along ❈

This little bug went out to play
Out on a little branch one day,
Watching him was so much fun
We took the branch before he could
    run.

We put it in this box so neat
And added some things for him to eat,
We'll study our bug for a day or two
And let him go when we're all through.

Who: All ages

How to Use It

Use this bug keeper to store insects and plants that **schoolagers** and **preschoolers** collect. Study the insects for a day or two, and then let them go. With help from adults, older children can learn more about the insect by reading, watching nature videos, and seeing similar specimens at a natural history museum. The bug keeper provides an opportunity for **toddlers** and **young preschoolers** to explore—with a sense of safety—things in the environment that they often fear. (It might even help some parents get over insect phobias.) Help the children look for things such as the number of legs, the kind of eyes, color and design on the body, body texture, and preferred food. A large magnifying glass will add much to this experience.

What It Does

The bug keeper helps children learn about and gain a respect for other living things. It provides the hands-on, concrete experience that makes the use of other resources—such as books and discussions—a richer, more meaningful learning experience for the child. The bug keeper promotes observation skills and language development. It may help some children overcome their fear of bugs. And, since it only uses recyclable items that parents can help supply, all the children can have their own bug keeper.

What You Need
- widemouthed clear plastic jar with lid
- scissors
- clean stocking or panty hose
- 2 twist-ties from bread bags or rubber bands

How to Make It

1. Cut two or three windows out of the sides of the jar.

2. Slip the jar into a leg of the stocking (the lighter the color and the finer the knit, the better). Cut off the foot and upper part of the stocking, leaving 6 inches at each end.

3. Gather the stocking to one side of the jar's bottom and fasten it with a twist-tie or rubber band. Gather insects and plants. Place the insects in the jar and cover with the lid. Fasten the top of the stocking with another twist-tie or rubber band.

Variation

For more bug-related ideas and activities, see the "Bugs Around Us Walk" chapter in *Open the Door Let's Explore More!* by Rhoda Redleaf (Redleaf Press, 1997).

Rhythm Shakers

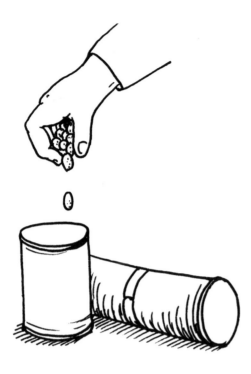

☀ Say-Along ☀

Listen to the noise I make
When I give this a little shake,
I can make the noise even louder
If I shake this a little harder.

We can play with these in our rhythm
band
And help the music sound just grand,
Do you know what we can do?
We'll dance and play a song for you.

Who: All ages

How to Use It

Infants will enjoy the noisy cause and effect these rhythm shakers create as they wave them about. **Toddlers** will begin to explore and experiment with the different sounds each shaker makes. **Preschoolers** and **schoolagers** will use them as rhythm instruments and sound effects. **Schoolagers** may also help make noisemakers for younger children by choosing different materials for different sounds and then assembling them.

What It Does

Shaking noisemakers reinforces infants' beginning realization that they can act upon their environment to make things happen (in this case, noise). Noisemakers also encourage pushing, grasping, and shaking movements. The shakers give toddlers a chance to discover how they can make different sounds by moving the shakers in different ways or by using different shakers. Shakers encourage music, rhythm, and dramatic expression in preschoolers and schoolagers. Making the instruments helps schoolagers gain an understanding of how different materials affect the sounds produced.

What You Need
- metal or plastic container and cover
- noise-making materials
- tape

How to Make It

1. Put a small amount of noise-making material into the container. Consider using buttons, small bells tied together with sturdy thread, dried beans, rice, popcorn, or pebbles.
2. Tape the cover securely in place.

Index